Those Wild Northwest Days

Second Edition

Twenty-five offbeat stories about the Pacific Northwest's pioneers and the towns they inhabited

Cheryl Landes

Tabby Cat Communications

Published in the United States by Tabby Cat Communications in Camas, WA

Cover design by Laura Stone and updated for the second edition by Cheryl Landes
Tabby Cat Communications logo design by Charlie Okada
Paperback inside pages design, layout, and index by Cheryl Landes
eBook conversion by HR Hegnauer
Photography by Cheryl Landes

Paperback ISBN: 979-8-9895450-4-9
eBook ISBN: 979-8-9895450-7-0
Library of Congress Control Number: 2025924942

This book is dedicated to

my grandparents

Vesta Beatrice Edmonds (1907-1974)
Richard Monroe Edmonds (1884-1970)

and

"Mom and Dad Landes"

Theresa Minerva Landes (1914-2003)
Alfred Valentine Landes (1907-2003)

Table of Contents

Preface

This is the second edition of *Those Wild Northwest Days*. I published the original version in June 2006. I've updated the second edition with new information and some corrections. My original preface is below, and it explains how I became interested in Northwest history and how the first edition transpired. I hope you enjoy reading these short stories.

I'm thinking about writing a series of these stories. The Pacific Northwest is full of fascinating stories, and I would love to share as many as possible. If you can recommend any places to explore or pioneers to research, please contact me.

Preface from 2006

This book has been almost 25 years in the making. When it started, I had no idea that I would become a fan of Northwest history or that I would even write a book about the subject. It's amazing how fate steers us in various directions in our lives.

My interest in Northwest history began during my sophomore year at Eastern Oregon State College (now Eastern Oregon University) in La Grande, a town of about 12,000 tucked away in the scenic Grande Ronde Valley in the state's northeast corner. My spring term schedule included a class focusing on the area's history. I was a general studies major, and my goal was to transfer to the University of Oregon to finish my journalism degree. The history class was a transfer elective. Our final assignment was to find an unusual person or town in northeastern Oregon and write a paper about it. The more unusual, the better.

After snooping around in the library and talking to friends and acquaintances, I found my topic: a ghost town called Greenhorn in the Blue Mountains. Three people still lived there but only in the summer. The winters were too harsh for their liking. I learned that Greenhorn had been a booming gold mining town from the late 1800s through the 1920s. That isn't very unusual in this corner of the state, though, for many gold mining towns were born and died during that period. What was unusual about Greenhorn was that at one time, it was a principality, a law unto itself. In other words, Greenhorn was a tiny country within the United States (see page 53 for more details).

Then I started learning more about the pioneers who lived there, their motivations for living there, and their struggles to survive in such a harsh environment. Their stories, hiding in old newspaper articles, unpublished typewritten texts shelved in local libraries, and in the memories of former residents, were fascinating—far more interesting than the dry, boring facts most commonly found in a history book. I wondered why more of these stories weren't easily accessible for others to enjoy. If others could read these stories, I thought, maybe more people would actually become interested in history.

Those thoughts simmered in the back of my mind as I wrote my paper about Greenhorn and, later for a different class, a paper about Hot Lake Sanatorium, nine miles southeast of La Grande. Back then, the sanatorium was another neglected site that was once known as a world-class resort (see pages 27–33). During the early 20th century, patients would come there seeking cures for their ailments by soaking in the lake's mineral waters. The resort's popularity began declining in the mid-1930s after its most famous physician, Dr. William Phy, died from polio. At the time I lived in La Grande, the owners of the property either didn't seem interested in renovating the deteriorating buildings or weren't able to invest the money into such a massive project. No one knew for sure. The resort appeared to be doomed, until David and Lee Manuel purchased the property. (David is a highly respected bronze sculptor who specializes in western art; Lee is a successful entrepreneur with a flair for promotion.) Now new life is breathing into the resort. An art gallery and gift shop opened there in November 2005, and David has already moved his bronze foundry into the restored wing from its original location in Joseph, Oregon, about 75 miles north of the lake. Restoration work continues at a fast, furious pace, and the couple plans to open the resort to guests sometime this year to coincide with the 100th anniversary of the construction of the main building, which is still standing.

My interest in Northwest history continued to grow after I transferred to the University of Oregon. Any time I could incorporate the subject into a class project, I would. After I graduated from the School of Journalism, I started working for the State of Oregon in Salem. The office where I worked was one block from the Oregon State Library, so during my lunch hours, I would skip eating and spend the 60 minutes browsing the card catalogs in the Northwest collection. My low-tech surfing washed up more fascinating stories about the pioneers and towns throughout the state. I was hooked.

After Tom, my husband, and I married and settled in Seattle, we began exploring the Northwest. On weekends and vacations, we followed back roads and hiking trails into small towns and abandoned mining camps. I gained a reputation with his family as someone who goes to the extreme in taking pictures. Our trips were not measured in miles per hour, but in pictures per mile. Tom didn't help matters any, for he would point out subjects that he thought should be captured on film. We both loved the outdoors and discovered together that we both enjoyed Northwest history.

I started transforming my research into articles. My first historical article appeared in *Old West* magazine in 1990. Since then, more than 100 of my articles have been published in newspapers, magazines, and journals throughout the United States and Canada. Twenty-five of those articles are featured as chapters in *Those Wild Northwest Days*. There's really no theme to this book, other than the chapters focus on towns and people in the Northwest from the 1860s through the 1920s, and the stories are lively and, hopefully, interesting for you to read. If I accomplish nothing else from publishing this book, I hope that it will spark your curiosity in Northwest history and encourage you to learn more about it.

Cheryl Landes
May 1, 2006

A Cat of a Different Feather

Baker City, Oregon

Thousands of stories exist about the lives of American pioneers, but few are told or written about pioneer cats.

Mouser was a cat that lived on the Carlile family farm at Upper Willow Creek near Baker City in northeastern Oregon. His life was the same as any average farm cat in 1878, until he became the target of a joke during an Indian raid.

At that time, Indian raids were common in northeastern Oregon. When tribes went on the warpath and began to raid the countryside, riders on horseback tried to warn their fellow settlers before the attack. The homeowners then fled, taking refuge wherever they could in the brush, timber, or mountains. They did not have time to gather their belongings.

When Indians moved in on Upper Willow Creek, the Carliles left Mouser in the house as they fled for safety. When they returned, they found the house ransacked, as expected. But they also saw a small, strange, four-footed creature dash past them. Feathers were scattered everywhere.

When Mr. Carlile managed to get near the animal, it meowed at him. It was Mouser!

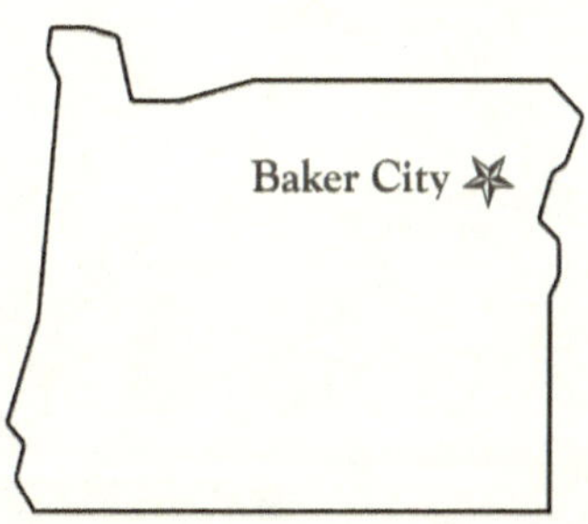

After a closer investigation, the Carliles unraveled the mystery of Mouser's new attire. When the Carliles fled, they left a sealed keg of molasses in the kitchen. It was now open. Apparently, the taste did not appeal to the Indians, so they grabbed Mouser, dunked him in the molasses, and turned him loose. As an added touch, it seemed, they ripped open the feather bed so the feathers would stick to the cat's body.

Of course, it was impossible to salvage either the molasses or the bed. But after a long, wild chase, the Carliles finally succeeded in catching Mouser. They sheared and bathed him, and eventually, he became a normal-looking cat again.

Fortunately, Mouser witnessed no more Indian raids. He lived out the rest of his life as a happy, carefree cat on Upper Willow Creek.

A Losing Battle Against Mother Nature

Sandon, British Columbia

When John Morgan ("Johnny") Harris heard about the rich silver strikes in southern British Columbia, he wanted in on the action. So, he traveled from the Coeur d'Alene area of Idaho to Slocan country, pitched a tent beside Carpenter Creek, staked a claim, and founded the town of Sandon in 1892. Sandon quickly became one of the largest communities in the interior of British Columbia. Twenty-nine hotels, 28 saloons, an opera house, stores, factories, mills, and two railroads served nearly 3,000 people.

Harris' fortunes grew as fast as the town. About the same time he founded Sandon, he formed a partnership with Fred T. Kelly. Together they purchased a group of claims that became the Reco Mine, which paid dividends of $200,000 in 1897. Harris also owned the Reco Hotel and a power plant that supplied the town's electricity.

But despite Harris' good fortune, Sandon seemed doomed from the beginning, thanks to its location. It followed a narrow valley surrounded by mountains, where avalanches and mudslides were common. Floods were another problem, because Carpenter Creek flowed through the center of town.

One of the first recorded disasters with casualties happened on March 5, 1898, at the Noble 5 Mine, two miles above town. The mine was built in a safe place, but miners had to cross a large slide area known as the Bluebird on their way to and from work. On that day, an avalanche buried two men on their way home from work. Volunteers came from Sandon, Cody, and the surrounding mines to dig but could not find the bodies until several days later. The Bluebird continued to take lives—sometimes one a year, sometimes two or more—throughout the boom years.

Another slide later that year involved William Bennett, Alex Forrest, and George Blanche, who leased the Mountain Con Mine at the head of Carpenter Creek, nine miles from Sandon. Since the mine was at an altitude of 7,500 feet, snow came early and stayed well into the summer. Each snowstorm caused avalanches because the surrounding mountains were almost sheer cliffs. That year the men stayed at the mine later in the season than usual because they found a small vein of silver-lead ore and were curious about its size.

At quitting time on November 11, a slide rumbled over the tunnel, sweeping Bennett and Blanche down the hillside. Forrest was not caught by the slide, so he began searching for his partners. He found Blanche barely conscious and groaning in pain. Although Forrest was much the smaller man, he somehow managed to carry Blanche to their cabin and put him to bed. Once Blanche was as comfortable as possible, Forrest left to look for Bennett. After a few hours with no luck, he returned to the cabin, checked on Blanche, and left to continue his search.

After 24 hours, Forrest had not returned to the cabin. Blanche began to worry that something had happened and decided to get help, despite his condition. The next morning he dressed as warmly as possible and started the journey to town. His injuries prevented him from walking very far, so he crawled most of the way. When he arrived in Sandon late that night, he was taken to the hospital. A search party organized to look for the two missing men, but snow fell so heavily that the search had to be stopped.

Neither Forrest's nor Bennett's bodies were found until the next summer. When Forrest was found, his hand was still clutching a light he had made by placing a candle in a jam can when he left to look for Bennett. An autopsy showed that Forrest died from a broken neck, probably when he fell on the trail. The autopsy report does not speculate on why he may have fallen.

Fires plagued Sandon, beginning in the spring of 1899, when a conflagration wiped out the town. Sources do not indicate the

Sandon in 1991. Carpenter Creek is at the left of this photo.

Three of the renovated buildings in Sandon in 2025. The Sandon Historical Museum is in the building at the right of this photo, and Carpenter Creek is in the foreground.

cause of the fire. Harris was also a victim; his hotel, the Reco, was completely destroyed. But like the other townsfolk, he started rebuilding as soon as the coals started cooling.

To reopen the Reco faster, he converted his pack-horse stable, which escaped the flames, into a plain, two-story box. Its front door opened to a board sidewalk under which flowed Carpenter Creek. When he finished, all the modern comforts and luxuries were inside: pink-and-blue floral carpets, heavy oak furniture, an indicator connecting bedrooms to the lobby desk, and a 14-foot mahogany bar topped with beveled mirrors.

Two hundred of Sandon's most prominent citizens were invited to the opening in September 1900, and soon after, the Reco dominated the town's social life. Some residents commented that Harris not only controlled the light and water plants and the local trade, but he was also in charge of the city's gossip. High-stakes stud-poker players gathered almost every night in the Reco's billiard room. Harris joined the games often and occasionally bet $50 on a single throw.

A second fire destroyed most of the business section on May 3, 1900. It started in the opera house and quickly spread to other frame buildings. Once again, the optimistic pioneers began rebuilding before the ashes cooled.

Klondike Silver Corporation, an active mining operation in Sandon.

The Slocan Mines historical marker in Sandon.

In 1906, a four-year-old boy playing with matches in his mother's bedroom started another fire. A slight breeze wafted a lace curtain over a lit match, and fire raced up the curtain, igniting the wallpaper. The frightened boy hid under the bed. By then, the house could not be saved. As the boy's parents and sister stood outside watching their house burn, his sister realized he was still in the house. She ran inside and managed to rescue him, but her hands were badly burned.

Volunteer firefighters fought the blaze to keep it from spreading into the main part of town. When the Kaslo and Slocan train arrived at Sandon that day, the train crew stopped to help the firefighters. At one time, they were forced to retreat so quickly that they left the hose cart and hoses to the fire. Although the blaze destroyed about 20 homes and the hospital, the only fatality was an excited dog that ran into a burning building and died when the door blew shut.

After World War I, Sandon's reputation as a boom town began slipping as quickly as the mudslides. Because many of the mines had been worked out, residents drifted away until only about 50 remained in the narrow valley, but Harris refused to leave. In 1926 at age 62, he wed Alma Lommatzch, a 25-year-old woman from Vulcan, Alberta, who had originally gone to Sandon to work in his office. It was his first and only marriage.

World War II brought new life to the town. After the Japanese attacked Pearl Harbor, Hawaii, on December 7, 1941, the Canadian government moved 12,000 Japanese-Canadians to southeastern British Columbia. Nine hundred fifty-three men, women, and children went to Sandon. The Harrises turned the Reco Hotel's big barroom into a general store and hired some of the Japanese. Alma managed the store, looked after the hotel, and served as the postmistress. Johnny continued tending the power plant on Carpenter Creek despite his failing health.

When the Japanese left at the end of the war, Sandon's fate as a ghost town was sealed. Johnny Harris still refused to leave, however, because he believed vast supplies of rich ores still lay deep in the mountains. The couple continued to live in the Reco Hotel and kept it open for guests until he died in 1953. His body was taken to Virginia for burial at his request. Alma sold most of the remaining assets in Sandon, and she lived in Silverton, British Columbia, until her death in 1988.

Two years after Johnny's death, the town of Sandon took another blow from Mother Nature. In June 1955, a wild thunderstorm struck at the height of the seasonal floods. Carpenter Creek burst its flume, pouring tons of rock and debris down the main street. Water carried the board sidewalk away while stores and buildings collapsed.

During Sandon's heyday, more than 300 mines operated in the area. Since 1892, more than $35 billion of silver in today's Canadian dollars ($24.9 billion US) have been produced there. Today, mining continues on a smaller scale.

Sandon's current population is six, which includes four humans and two cats, a black American Bombay named Eli and a gray tabby named Jack. The cats hang out in a catio next door to a concession stand, The few buildings that are still standing have been renovated, and one houses a museum. The city hall building has a gift shop that sells T-shirts and sweatshirts, books, jewelry, and other souvenirs The hydroelectric plant is still in operation, and it's open for tours.

The catio, where two cats hang out in Sandon.

Above: The Silversmith Powerhouse in Sandon, which opened in 1897. It's the oldest continuous operating hydroelectric plant in Canada. Below: Inside the hydroelectric plant.

A Town Without a Home

Randolph, Oregon

In the spring of 1852, Indians prospecting on a beach north of the mouth of the Coquille River made the first discovery of gold on the Oregon Coast. They stumbled upon a finely particled supply unevenly scattered in the thick, black sands where a small creek entered the ocean. Sometimes they found only a trace of color; other times, a panful of sand yielded from eight to 10 dollars.

The following summer, the Indians sold their claim for $20,000 to two brothers, "Big Mac" and "Little Mac" McNamera, who removed an estimated $100,000 worth of the yellow flakes.

Meanwhile, somewhere nearby, Joe Crowley quietly recovered a mule load of gold and left in the middle of the night. Unfortunately, his wealth wouldn't last, as was generally the case with miners who became rich overnight. He either squandered his wealth or was fleeced of it, dying a poor man without even a mule.

Despite Crowley's silence about his find, the news of gold at the beach spread, and by the summer of 1853, prospectors flocked there from as far away as San Francisco. More than 1,000 men staked claims on the beach for miles north and south. Soon a town was thrown together on a bluff against a somber background of densely wooded hills overlooking the beach.

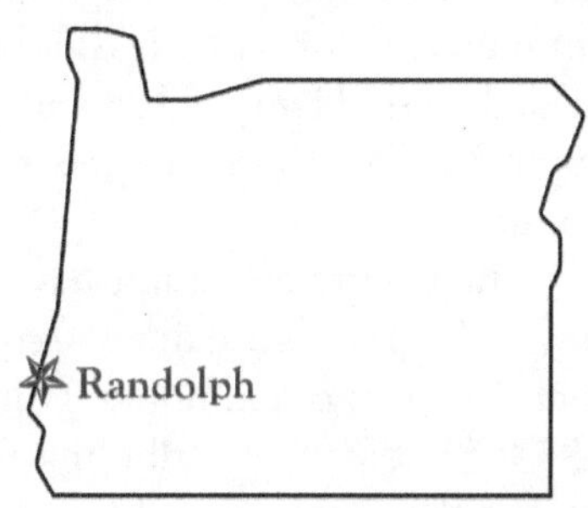

Within the first few weeks of its establishment, the town sprawled with saloons, restaurants,

Whiskey Run Creek, which continues enticing amateur prospectors. The author often spots abandoned sluice boxes there during her beachcoming adventures.

stores, hotels, cabins, tents, and a jumble of board and log houses with shake roofs, stone and mud chimneys, oiled-paper windows, and puncheon floors. A trail was built to Coos Bay, 27 miles northeast, which connected the site with ocean transportation.

Some of the settlers named the site Randolph after John Randolph, a U.S. representative from Roanoke, Virginia, who was remembered for "fluttering" Philadelphia in 1803 with the happy announcement that he had fathered a child out of wedlock. He also dueled with Henry Clay and popularized the term "doughface," applied to Northern congressmen who voted with Southern slave-holding interests.

The tribute could not have been more appropriate, because the town of Randolph gained a colorful reputation. So did the beach that the town called home. During the Coos County Gold Rush of 1853–55, the creek dribbling into the Pacific was named Whiskey Run, either because of the miners and settlers transporting whiskey barrels to the beach (a "whiskey run"), the heavy drinking in the area, or the creek suggested "firewater" to some of the thirstier prospectors. According to one legend, the amount of booze consumed there outweighed the gold recovered. The label for the creek was later tacked onto the beach as well.

About that time, a story about hidden gold evolved. Two miners who made a rich strike buried a five-gallon can of gold dust beneath a tree in the woods behind Whiskey Run Beach and left for supper. While they were gone, a forest fire swept the mining district, leaving thousands of black-charred snags and stumps. The fire obliterated all evidence of where the gold was hidden. After they returned, the miners searched for weeks before giving up. No records of the gold's recovery exist.

During its boom years, Randolph rivaled Jacksonville, the most famous gold town in the history of western Oregon. But Randolph's fame would not last long. Mother Nature took over in the spring of 1854, unleashing her fury on the beach. A violent storm erased most of the gold-bearing sands and buried sluice boxes and shafts. Some miners stayed, hoping for the ocean to bring a new supply of wealth, while others left for new fields.

One man who didn't wait was "Coarse-Gold" Johnson. He tried

Whiskey Run Beach, the original townsite of Randolph, Oregon.

The Coquille River Lighthouse, also known as the Bullards Beach Lighthouse. This site was one of Randolph's many temporary homes before the town's decline.

his luck a few miles south of the Bullards Beach Lighthouse and found it was in his favor. Word of his fortune spread to Randolph, and the entire population rushed to settle around the new claim, taking the town's name with them.

At this point, accounts of Randolph's fate conflict. One states when the gold supplies shrank, so did Randolph. Two years after the town was founded, it was almost deserted. Then, in the 1860s, the town was moved farther inland along the Coquille River.

The other version, a bit more detailed, appears to be more accurate. On August 18, 1859, Randolph was recorded in the annals of the National Archives in Washington, D.C., as a post office. (Old-time post offices moved from one place to another according to the residence of the postmaster.) According to this account, the change of postmasters moved the location of Randolph three times after the Whiskey Run storm. George Wasson, the first postmaster, lived at the Fahy Farm near the Bullards Ferry. On April 20, 1863, John Hamblock succeeded Wasson, and Randolph went to Bullards

Beach. All the locations were within a few miles of each other.

About three miles upstream from the Bullards Ferry, Adam Pershbaker opened a store on the north bank of the Coquille River, and on December 7, 1871, he became the Randolph postmaster. The town's name migrated to the store, where business flourished for more than 20 years.

That site became Randolph's final resting place. It gradually began to lose its importance as Prosper, a new town five miles southwest, attracted residents interested in working in the fish cannery, shipyards, and sawmills. Pershbaker also packed and moved there, reopened the store and post office, and left the name Randolph behind.

Today, Randolph has two buildings and a road sign bearing its name. Whiskey Run and Bullards Beach are popular attractions for tourists and beachcombers, and occasionally, people struck with gold fever bring sluice boxes or pans along and try their luck at recovering morsels of wealth the old-time prospectors left behind.

Present-day Randolph, Oregon.

Another War Between the States

Oregon vs. Washington

American history books devote a lot of space to the story of the Civil War, also known as the War Between the States. However, none mention the Sand Island War, a Northwestern version of the Civil War that occurred between Oregon and Washington in 1896.

Back then, Sand Island was a small piece of land in the mouth of the Columbia River—a menace to navigators but a blessing to fishermen. Navigators dreaded sailing in this area, because constant erosion and silt deposits continually changed the shape and location of the island. Fishermen saw the waters surrounding Sand Island as a gold mine. Average salmon catches ranged from 300 to 500 tons each season, the largest in the world.

This vast fish supply lured fishermen from Oregon and Washington who hoped to gain larger shares of the catch. Their desires started the war.

Three hundred commercial gillnetting fishermen from Oregon sailed to Sand Island and destroyed buildings and equipment used by fishermen in Ilwaco, Washington, a few miles north. The Oregon gillnetters, who fished by dropping nets in the sea from small crafts, claimed the Washington fishermen caught more fish because they attached nets to pilings set near the shoreline.

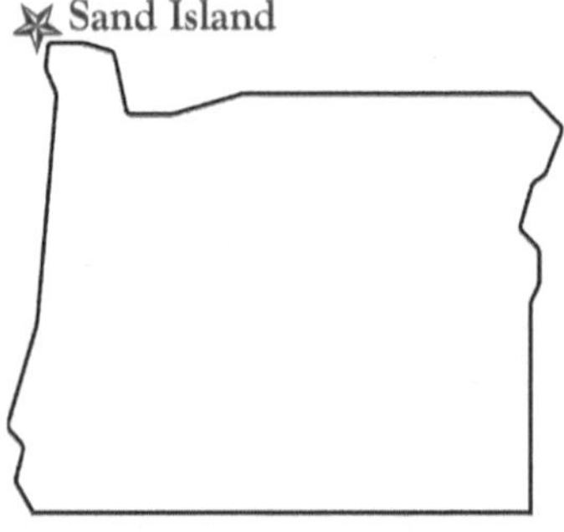

The accusation angered the Washington fishermen, because

they didn't use pilings to anchor their nets. Instead, each 1,400-foot net was attached to a team of 10 to 12 horses that steadied one end while a crew riding in a skiff, pulled by a tug, uncurled the other end and cast it into the sea. The tug then pulled the net shoreward as its crew worked to prevent tangling. When the net reached shallow water, beachcombers ran into the water to tie the ends together and keep the fish from jumping out of the net. Teams of horses drug the net onto the beach.

As soon as the net hit the beach, the ends were released. The salmon were removed from the net immediately, loaded onto wagons, and transported to the dock, where a scow carried the catch to canneries at Ilwaco and Astoria, Oregon.

Without equipment and buildings to shelter their horses and men during the fishing season, the Washington fishermen could no longer work. They left Sand Island and asked Ilwaco Sheriff Tom Roney for help in protecting their seining sites. Because the island was out of his jurisdiction, he wired a request to Governor John McGraw. The governor responded on April 10 by sending 60 National Guardsmen, led by Captain Frank Adams, to patrol the waterfront on the Washington side of the Columbia River.

Sheriff Roney described the fishermen's duel to Captain Adams and suggested if Washington exerted control over Sand Island, the dispute would end. Captain Adams agreed and authorized immediate occupation.

Captain Adams' decision, based on his knowledge of the ownership of the island, was made too hastily. Sand Island became the property of Oregon when the state was admitted to the union in 1859, but the state gave the island to the federal government in 1864. At that time, President Abraham Lincoln issued a proclamation preserving Sand Island for military purposes. When the federal government discovered the profits from salmon 16 years later, it began leasing seining sites to commercial fishermen.

Therefore, Captain Adams needed to consult federal authorities for permission to occupy the island. He didn't.

When the excited Washington National Guard troops stormed the island with their bayonets fixed, they found it empty. During the next two weeks, they stopped fishing craft, fired warning shots, settled down to garrison duty, and named their new home Fort Finnstopper.

The routine was boring, so when the guardsmen were off duty, they visited the spacious grounds at the Cape Disappointment Lighthouse and made free use of supplies.

Soon the lighthouse keeper caught them and complained to his superior, the chief of the Portland Lighthouse District. The chief asked the commanding officer, General Otis at the Vancouver, Washington, barracks, for help.

General Otis immediately telegraphed Major David Hunter Kenzie at the Fort Canby, Oregon, gun batteries, Fifth U.S. Artillery.

"Get the Washington National Guard off Sand Island—by force if necessary," his message said. "The island is federal property, not state!"

Major Kenzie armed 26 U.S. Army soldiers with 15 rounds of ammunition apiece and led them on a moonlit attack on the Sand Island garrison, Fort Finnstopper.

As the men confronted the Washington National Guard, Captain Adams drew his sword.

Major Kenzie faced Captain Adams and demanded, "Captain, by what authority are you occupying this island?"

"By virtue of the authority invested in me by the governor of the state of Washington!" Captain Adams shouted.

"Are you aware that you are occupying a federal government reserve?" Major Kenzie asked.

"I am," Captain Adams retorted. "But my orders are to protect the lives and property of the citizens of the state of Washington!"

"I am the duly authorized agent of the United States Government; as such I will allow you and your men 20 minutes to vacate. In the event of your failure to do so, my orders are to place the detachment on Sand Island under arrest!" Major Kenzie ordered.

Captain Adams paused, returned his sword to its scabbard, and ordered his troops to leave for Ilwaco.

Oregonians across the river became furious when they heard about the presence of federal troops on Sand Island, because their fishermen couldn't get near the good salmon fishing drifts around the island.

On June 15, Oregon Governor William Lord sent 400 National Guard officers and troops from Multnomah County to Astoria with orders to protect the interests of the state's fishermen. The atmosphere grew tense as they set boat patrols around Sand Island.

The dispute went as far as the Supreme Court, and in 1908, Oregon prevailed. When the north and south jetties were built on the Columbia River in 1932, Sand Island was covered with water. Over the years, interest in the area faded because of the dwindling salmon runs caused by the dams built on the Columbia River. In 1950, Oregon and Washington signed an interstate compact, which formally ended the conflict.

Today, Sand Island is two islands that were created by shifting alluvial deposits. The main island, 600 feet from the southern tip of the Long Beach Peninsula near the A jetty and U.S. Coast Guard Station at Cape Disappointment in Washington, is approximately 800 acres. East Sand Island is 62 acres located a mile west of Chinook, Washington. It's a popular place for birds to feed on salmon migrating to the Pacific Ocean.

The main island rarely has visitors. Occasionally a windsurfer rides the waves nearby, or boaters from Ilwaco or Chinook dock to beachcomb.

A view of the mouth of the Columbia River from the Astoria Column in Astoria, Oregon. This stretch of the river forms the Oregon-Washington state border.

Babylon of the West

Ruby, Washington

Sometime during the late 1880s, a newcomer drove a buckboard at a gallop into a settlement that became known as Ruby. He wore a white plug hat, which tempted a marksman to put a bullet through it. After the greenhorn recovered from his fright, the marksman offered to buy him a drink and said, "I believe I'd get a regular hat. That plug is so attractive that some other guy who ain't such a good shot may take a chance on it."

Episodes like this one were common in Ruby, a roaring mining community in northcentral Washington. It grew practically overnight after the United States opened the Colville Indian Reservation for settlement. In 1887, quartz ledges bearing pockets of silver and small amounts of gold were discovered near Salmon Creek. Miners and prospectors with dreams of instant wealth arrived from all over the Northwest. Population estimates during the peak of the boom ranged from 600 to 1,000.

Ruby was perhaps known more for its immorality than its silver; in fact, the town was so wild that outsiders nicknamed it the "Babylon of the West." Saloons, gambling houses, and brothels dominated the social scene. "This is a healthy country," one miner wrote. "I have been here two years and there has not been a natural death yet."

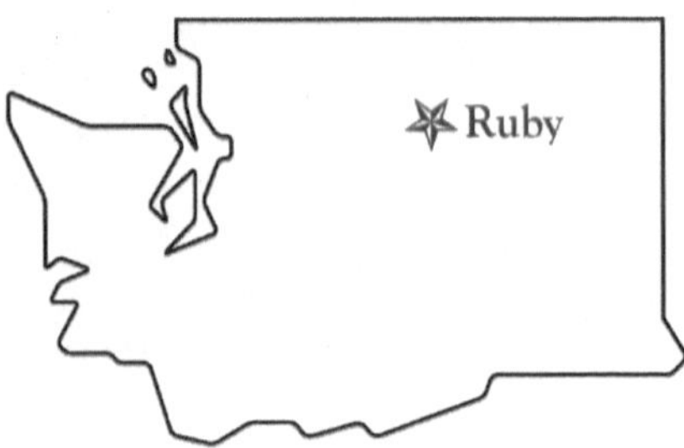

Shootings were common. In an interview for *The Seattle Times,* pioneer Ed Bown recalled attending a Fourth of July celebration in Ruby. An Indian named Pokemiakin was arrested for stealing a valuable race horse. Bullets flew while he tried to flee, and the animal was shot out from under him before he was captured.

On another occasion, miners shot out the front windows of Billie Darwin's hotel when Jonathan Bourne, one of the owners of the largest mine in Ruby, was staying there. He refused to raise the miners' pay.

Guy Waring, another pioneer, recalled a bloodier dispute in his book, *My Pioneer Past.* Late one night, an unruly drunken citizen tried to enter the town's main brothel. The madam of the house, annoyed at being disturbed, refused him admittance. The man became angry and took a swing at her. Then the madam, who was known for always wanting to have the last word in an argument, returned to her room, grabbed her revolver, and shot him through the heart. The man died instantly.

The man's body was found crumpled on the steps outside the brothel, and before the sheriff could be persuaded to investigate, the madam had already boarded the stage for Spokane Falls. She knew as soon as another scandal developed, she could return unnoticed and reopen her business.

Ruby townsite in northcentral Washington.

Historical marker at the abandoned Ruby townsite.

"After I listened to a group of citizens expound the merits of the case," Waring wrote, "I gained a still better idea of the level of morality one could expect to find in Ruby. No one cared much about the actual facts of the murder. The chief point of dispute was whether the madame had taken a previous dislike to her unwelcomed client because of the damage he had done to her staff of girls—for it was generally known in Ruby, I learned, that the gentleman's much-discussed limp had been caused by neither infantile paralysis, rheumatism, nor any other common form of affliction or accident!"

Because of the colorful characters in town, public celebrations were popular. One private event that soon became highly publicized happened on Christmas Eve 1887. While the miners were happily spending their wages on liquor in the town's largest saloon, news came that a baby boy was just born at George W. Carpenter's home. The infant was the first white boy born in Okanogan County.

These customers appointed a delegation of "three wise men" to call on George and carry him off to the bar to be toasted. At the height of the rowdy tribute, George was hoisted to the counter and asked to name his son Ruby. In return for honoring the town, George would be rewarded with a city lot. The crowd took up a collection to purchase the land, and presented the deed at Arthur Ruby Carpenter's christening—a champagne celebration.

Livelier festivities occurred when Ruby became the first county seat of Okanogan County. Until 1888, the Okanogan country was part of Stevens County. The territorial legislature that year adopted a measure creating Okanogan County and naming three temporary county commissioners (one of whom was Waring) to organize the new government, appoint its first officers, and select a temporary county seat. The commissioners met at John Perkins' ranch on Johnson Creek, four miles north Ruby, on March 6, 1888.

Although Ruby hadn't been named the county seat yet, many residents started celebrating. Waring described the scene. "It was an occasion I shall never forget. The people of Ruby, hearing of the meeting, all turned out to hold a noisy celebration in our honor. Whores, thieves, and drunkards, and other notorious citizens of the mining town were on hand some time before the oath of office was administered. They were of course agreeably drunk, and serenaded us so loudly that it was difficult for anybody inside the ranch house to hear himself speak."

During its 11-month period as the county seat, Ruby's government headquarters was a small shack; records were kept in ordinary notebooks. Liquor licenses were the primary source of revenue and, because the county didn't have a safe, treasurer E.C. Sherman put the $1,800 he received from taxes into an empty baking powder can and buried it on his ranch.

The question of selecting a permanent location for the county seat appeared on the ballot later in 1888. Conconully received the honor, and the transfer was completed in February 1889.

Ruby never became the second Comstock as some geologists predicted. In 1893, the boom ended when silver prices fell sharply and the town died quickly. It was deserted by 1899. Today, a historical marker and a few foundations, overgrown with grass, remain as a reminder of the bustling mining town once known as the "Babylon of the West."

Present-day Conconully, Washington.

Blood on the Junipers

Prineville, Oregon

On March 15, 1882, A.H. Crooks and his son-in-law, Stephen J. Jory, spent the morning blazing some lines of government land in the edge of the timber by Grizzly Butte, northwest of Prineville, Oregon. The land bordered Lucius Langdon's ranch near the head of lava-lined Willow Creek. Crooks and Jory worked throughout the morning, despite a dispute about property lines between their family and Langdon. At noon, they left their axes leaning against a big tree near Langdon's barn and went home for lunch.

When they returned that afternoon, Langdon shot and killed them. Then he jumped on a horse for a hasty escape.

Later that same day, Garret Maupin, a Trout Creek rancher who happened to be riding by the Willow Creek ranches, found Crooks' and Jory's bodies and rode to Prineville to spread the news of the murders. Prineville and the surrounding ranches were a part of Wasco County at that time, and the only law officer in the area was Deputy Sheriff J.L. Luckey. The closest police force was in The Dalles, 117 miles north.

Langdon was the obvious suspect. Within minutes, a loosely organized but law-abiding posse left Prineville, following shortcuts to Langdon's ranch. Crooks' and Jory's bodies lay on the ground. There was no trace of Langdon.

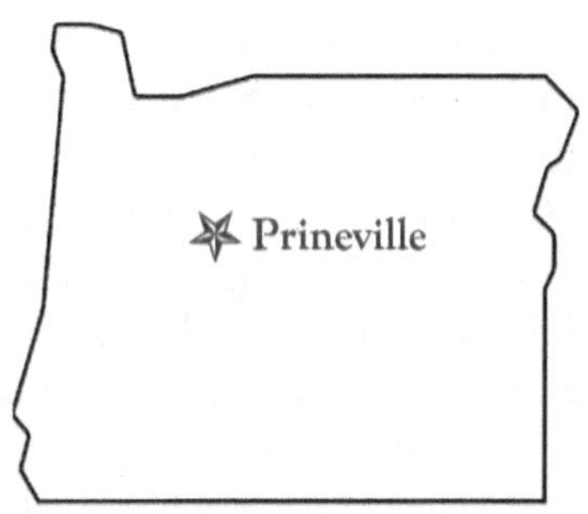

A second posse that materialized the same night on the Langdon ranch grew into a vigilante gang that would dictate rule from the saddle for the next two years. Organized formally as a "stock association," these men operated outside the law, riding bloody trails and dusty streets to seek revenge on anyone they did not like or who threatened them. Few people challenged the gang's authority for fear of their lives.

Before the vigilantes' reign ended, 11 men were either dead or missing, including Crooks and Jory. Those who died met their fate by a gun, a rope, or both.

The night after Crooks and Jory were murdered, some of the vigilante leaders suspected Langdon might have fled to the home of his brother on Mill Creek, 17 miles north of Prineville. Five men rode there that night, returning with word that Langdon had run away from the house and disappeared in the darkness when a barking dog warned of their approach.

Nearly 24 hours later, James Blakely and some of his companions—all opposed to the vigilantes—rode to Langdon's ranch house. The dog barked again. "I saw Langdon mount a white horse in front of the house, jump the horse over a ditch, and start for the road," Blakely said in an interview in *The Oregonian*. "We carried rifles and pistols, but there wasn't any occasion for gun play. I called out for him to stop and he rode right up to me. Mrs. Langdon was at the door of the house, screaming."

Blakely identified himself to Mrs. Langdon. Her husband and his captors entered the house and waited while Mrs. Langdon prepared supper. After supper, Blakely notified the Crooks and Jory families that Langdon had been taken prisoner. A warrant had been issued for Langdon's hired hand, W.H. Harrison, also a suspect, but the posse did not arrest him because Blakely saw him in Prineville at the time of the shooting.

After a long ride around Grizzly Mountain, the posse returned to Prineville with Langdon after midnight. They turned him over to Luckey, who took him to a hotel. Meanwhile, despite his alibi, Harrison had been arrested also.

At daylight on March 17, 1882, the wild ringing of the Prineville school bell awakened Blakely. His wife called from the window that a crowd was milling in the street. "They're carrying the body of a man in a red shirt!" she cried.

"That's Harrison!" Blakely exclaimed in anger.

Shortly before the bell sounded, the vigilantes seized Harrison at the hotel and dragged him through the streets behind a galloping horse while people watched in horror through doors and windows. The race ended at the Crooked River iron bridge, where Harrison was hanged. Langdon had already been shot and killed in the hotel.

Two stories of what actually had happened at the hotel that night emerged. In a letter to Sheriff Storrs of Wasco County, Deputy Sheriff Luckey gave his version of the double lynching. "Blakely woke me up (about 2 a.m.) saying they had captured Langdon and wanted to turn him over to me. I went down to the stable office where they had him, put the shackles on him, took him into the hotel, had a good fire built, and told Langdon to get some sleep on the lounge. I sat down by the stove to guard him. The town was soon aroused. Quite a number of men came in to see Langdon, I suspect through morbid curiosity. W.C. Foren, deputy marshal, came in and stayed with me. Harrison went to bed, and about 4 a.m. got up and sat by the stove.

"As I was sitting at the stove with my back to the front door, the door was suddenly opened and I was caught and thrown backwards on the floor and firmly held while my eyes were blindfolded. Immediately a pistol was fired rapidly five or six times.

"I heard someone groan, and at the same time the firing ceased. Harrison was hurried from the room. I could tell it was him by his cries. The doors were closed and I was allowed to get up. I went to Langdon and found him dead. I looked around and saw a masked man standing at each door, warning by ominous signs that no one was to leave the room. As soon as they were satisfied that Langdon was dead, they left.

"At daylight I took some men to help search for Harrison, and found him hanging from a banister of the Crooked River iron bridge."

The other version comes from Blakely, who recounted a story told by Leo Freid, a store man who was in the hotel that night. Freid did not witness the murder of Langdon, but he heard a conversation that led to Harrison's death. According to Freid, when things had quieted after the vigilantes shot Langdon, Harrison and the vigilantes were sitting by the stove talking about Langdon, Harrison said, "Well, he was always good to me."

Those words angered the vigilantes. They grabbed Harrison, pulling him from the hotel while he begged for his life. The vigilantes tied a rope around Harrison's neck. One of them mounted a horse, dragging Harrison down the street toward the bridge.

Blakely believed Luckey knew who killed Harrison and protected their identities in his letter to the Wasco County sheriff. "Of course I wasn't at the hotel and I can't say, as an eyewitness, that the men weren't masked," Blakely said, "but I do know that the horse wasn't marked. It was generally known whose horse it was and who rode it. The deputy sheriff had a strong personal reason to shield that man. It just so happened that the horse was one that I had sold not long before."

The events of that night banded the vigilantes into a tightly knit, brazen group. They started sending threatening letters marked with crossbones and skulls to what Blakely describes as "a good many number" of men, mostly law-abiding citizens whose only crime was opposing the vigilantes.

The gang gained a stronger foothold after October 1882, when the state legislature voted to carve Crook County out of Wasco County, effective the following January. Two of Governor Zenas Ferry Moody's major county appointments were sympathetic to the vigilantes. As county judge, he named S.G. Thompson, brother of Colonel William "Bud" Thompson, a leader of the vigilantes; and as treasurer, Gus A. Winckler, a storekeeper who tried to convince Blakely's brother to join in the Langdon-Harrison lynching.

Through their so-called stock association, the vigilantes tried to regulate central Oregon pastureland by stating that anyone who wanted to ride on the range had to get an order from them. Blakely openly defied that "policy" in front of the Barnes boys, some relatives heavily involved with the gang. "I was born in this Oregon country and I'll be damned if anyone is going to tell me where I can go out after my own stock," he told them. Blakely bought five six-shooters—two .41 Colts and three .32 Smith and Wessons—and gave them to his riders. After that, the vigilantes never attempted to enforce their policy.

Christmas Eve 1882 was another bloody night in Prineville. The drama began as Al Schwartz, who was raised near Salem, played cards with his back to a window in Burmeister's saloon. He felt a draft and noticed someone had opened the window. After he closed it and sat down again, someone outside shot him fatally in the back of the neck, directly through the glass.

Later that night, the vigilantes lured two young men named Sidney Huston and Charles Luster to the Barnes ranch and hanged them from a juniper tree. The gang charged that one of the youngsters had planned to steal some horses, but opponents of the vigilantes had a different explanation for the lynchings. They said Luster, a jockey, agreed to throw a race but then bet $60 on his horse and won.

After those murders, someone wrote a boastful account to the local newspapers, claiming credit for the vigilantes, praising their performance, and asserting Schwartz, Huston, and Luster were members of a gang that had been running stolen livestock out of central Oregon. The letters also indicated Schwartz defied the vigilantes.

Steve Staats, a member of a pioneer family, became the next victim, shot under mysterious circumstances at his ranch near Powell Butte, 11 miles southwest of Prineville. Staats openly condemned the gang for lynching Harrison. About the same time Staats died, rancher Shorty Davis, whom Blakely described as "a nice little fellow," disappeared. Blakely and some of his friends looked for Davis' body but never found it.

Shortly after the Huston-Luster lynching, Mike Mogan and J.M. "Mossy" Barnes were playing cards in Dick Graham's saloon and started arguing. Barnes pulled a gun and held it on Mogan.

"Why, Mossy, you wouldn't shoot me." Mogan said quietly.

Barnes responded by pulling the trigger.

Although Mogan was hit hard, he managed to rise and walk across the street to pick up his gun at the livery stable. He fell in the street on the way back.

Blakely talked to Mogan the day after the shooting. Mogan said, "Him [*sic*], I hope to God I get well. I know who done [*sic*] this, and I'll take care of them fellows. That was Bud (William) Thompson's gun that Mossy used. I saw it often when I was working for him."

Mogan's wish to recover did not come true. He died several days later.

The violence was still going on a year later. On December 18, 1883, William Thompson killed Frank Mogan, Mike's brother, while he stood in the Kelley saloon with his head and elbows propped on the bar. Frank didn't have a chance to defend himself, because Thompson walked up from behind and shot him in the back of the neck.

In his book, *Reminiscences of a Pioneer*, William Thompson later attempted to justify the shooting by claiming Frank had threatened his life. Thompson said on the day of the shooting, he heard Frank was in town gunning for him. "I determined to settle the matter one way or the other at our first meeting," Thompson wrote. "The test came sooner than I anticipated. On seeing me he attempted to draw his gun, but was too slow, and fell with more than one bullet through his body."

The slayings of the Mogan brothers finally brought a climax to the vigilantes' long rule. The break came when a group of Crook County residents, headed by Blakely, openly defied them.

As usual, open opposition like this was not ignored. The vigilantes warned, "If Jim Blakely doesn't watch his step, he will be going up the hill feet first some day [*sic*]." The "hill" was the pioneer cemetery on a flat just north of town overlooking Crooked River Valley.

Blakely and his men adopted the name, "Moonshiners," because they kept lookout stations at night when the vigilantes were most active. Old-timers said one of the stations was on top of an early-day flour mill in Prineville.

The Moonshiners were not a gun-slinging, night-riding outfit. They were established Prineville residents who realized their newly formed Crook County was off to a bad start. The new posse soon expanded into an organization of about 75 men who participated in shaping Oregon's new Ochoco frontier.

One day, the Moonshiners decided to make a show of force by riding down Prineville's main street fully armed and astride fine horses. The little community had never seen such a display of power, and residents agreed this militia had the law on its side and determined men in the saddle. These men were not masked and were recognized by their neighbors. A group of vigilantes sat in one of the saloons and watched this "cavalry of Crooked River" pass. The Moonshiners dared them to come out, but they refused.

That ride by Jim Blakely and his armed men through Prineville's dusty main street ended the rule of the vigilantes. When the first regular election was held in Crook County in June 1884, practically all who opposed the vigilantes were elected, most of them sworn to rid the area of the masked riders. The vigilantes did not dare to apologize openly for their reign because of the murders they had committed, but in later years, through unsigned letters and remarks to friends, they declared their stern rule was necessary because no law and order existed in Crook County before the June 1884 election.

Backers of the vigilantes also noted that Prineville had only county deputies to enforce the law during its early days. Even when Crook County was created in 1882, its only law officer, except for a marshal in Prineville, was a deputy. News of the Crooks and Jory murders and the Langdon-Harrison lynching did not reach Sheriff Storrs in The Dalles until 10 days later. No attempts were made to send the sheriff either a telegram or message by express rider.

After the vigilantes made their last ride, Crook County became a rapidly developing livestock-raising area, its serenity disturbed only briefly by a range war. Residents of Prineville were proud of the vast ranges beyond the hills and referred to the region as "the West's last frontier."

Prineville city hall and courthouse on the town's main street.

Boom Times in Republic

Republic, Washington

At 12:01 a.m. on February 21, 1896, the federal government opened the Colville Indian Reservation in the northeast corner of Washington for mineral entry. Within hours, excited prospectors shot guns and shouted, "Eureka!" to celebrate the discovery of their first veins of gold.

The news rekindled the gold fever that had struck other western towns. Hungry prospectors began to arrive at Eureka Gulch, slowly at first, but faster as word spread. Tents gave way to permanent frame buildings, and the town of Republic was born.

Estimates of Republic's population during the boom years range from 5,000 to 10,000. Money flowed easily, as did the liquor. Although alcohol was banned during the first two years of the town's existence, bootleggers managed to supply plenty.

After the ban was lifted, 22 saloons, along with two dance and gambling halls, opened to provide entertainment for the miners. One saloon at the edge of town along the route miners followed to and from the mines, drew customers with a well-placed sign. On one side, they saw, "last chance," which targeted the men heading to work. On the other side, those returning home saw the words, "first chance."

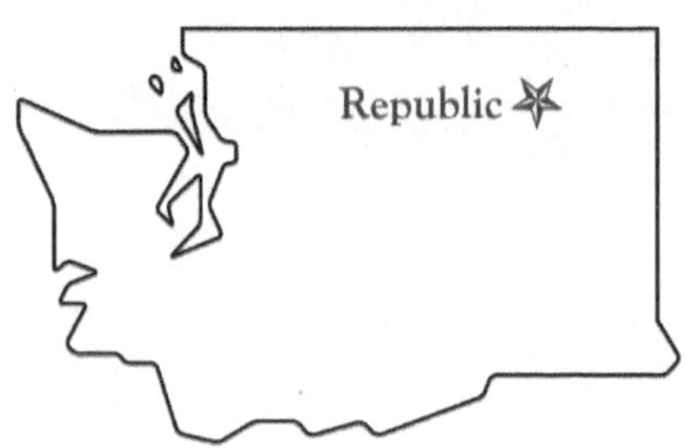

Each customer had his own bottle of whiskey on the back bar of his favorite saloon. When he entered and lined up against the bar, the bartender put the bottle and a glass in front of him. The customer either filled the glass or skipped the formalities and drank from the bottle. One tough old lawman, nicknamed "Black Jack," cut a chew from his tobacco plug, turned up his bottle, and swallowed four or five swigs before coming up for air. While the whiskey settled and the chew started working, he lit a big, black Havana cigar.

With so many customers, bartenders faced challenges in remembering the drinks their customers preferred, but it was worse when the bar ran out of a favorite drink before the next freight wagon was due.

George Moody, who operated a saloon during Republic's boom years, recalled one of these moments. A customer, Jack McDermott, had only two drinks left in his bottle, and Moody encouraged him to try another brand. McDermott consented and Moody poured a shot. As was his custom, McDermott downed the drink in one swallow, and his response to the taste can't be printed here. Fortunately, McDermott's favorite whiskey arrived the next day.

After this episode, Moody and his bartender tried an experiment: they would determine whether miners could really identify different brands of whiskey by taste alone. They chose a man who had sworn he could tell the difference, and when his bottle was empty, the bartender refilled it with another brand. When the customer gulped a shot, he said, "Man, that is whiskey!"

Moody and the bartender got the same results, even after substituting four different brands, and after testing another so-called expert. They concluded as long as they poured a different brand in the old bottle, the customer couldn't tell the difference.

Gambling was also a favorite pastime. The most popular games in Republic were faro, roulette, dice, draw poker, and five-card stud. Living was high and gamblers took the loss of a few thousand dollars in stride. After all, with daily assays going as high as $1,260 per ton, miners thought they could replenish these losses in a day or two. Less enthusiastic gamblers, who played more for pleasure than money, liked two-handed cribbage or heart solo, the forerunner of pinochle.

As in many mining boom towns, there were few women in Republic, and they mostly worked the cribs. Because of the shortage of women, dance hall owners had to find alternatives for the thousands of men without partners on Saturday nights. The most common solution was to have half of the men volunteer to dress as women. Their attire was simply a brightly colored ribbon tied around their heads with a huge bow in back.

Not everyone in Republic succeeded in mining. Those who didn't found other occupations, generally using skills they gained elsewhere. Examples include the Republic Brewery, two soda pop manufacturers, two Havana cigar makers, and the Straight Edge Razor Company. Others delivered or sold freight.

U.E. Fries, a pioneer who spent most of his life in Okanogan, Washington, recalled his experiences as a freighter in his book, *From Copenhagen to Okanogan.* "During the late nineties," he wrote, "I freighted my own produce to the boom town of Republic...When I did not have a full load of my own produce...I would buy enough apples, peaches, tomatoes, and melons from other settlers to fill out my load. The freight rate from Brewster to Republic, which were, roughly, a hundred miles apart, was about one and one-fourth cents a pound, but I could not make as much money by charging that rate as I would by buying produce and selling it. I have bought fifty-pound boxes of apples for a dollar and then sold them for two and a half dollars a box—and sometimes for as much as four dollars.

"My loads averaged three thousand pounds, and I drove twenty-five to thirty miles a day. I made the round trip of two hundred and ten miles in seven days. This included one day spent selling my produce."

When the easier supplies of gold diminished, Republic's population dropped significantly, but the town remained alive. Approximately 1,000 people live there today, and gold mining continues on a smaller scale. Republic has the only active gold mine in Washington.

Republic's main street.

Buckaroo Bubble Bath

Soap Lake, Washington

As long as cowboys have ridden the range, they have enjoyed two forms of relaxation at the end of a long, hard day's work—eating hearty dinners and spinning yarns around the campfire. In one of their tales, a buckaroo dies and is buried in the dark brown mud along the Soap Lake shoreline in the central Washington desert. A few days later, he surprises his former companions when he rides into their main camp on a cayuse he found on the range. When they ask him about his miraculous recovery, he says the minerals from the lake's waters seeped into his body and revived him.

The cowboys who drove cattle and sheep through central Washington must have believed the story because they chose Soap Lake as one of their regular camping spots. They bathed their horses and blankets in its alkali waters to prevent saddle sores and used the mud to cure snake bites. When they moved sheep from one ranch to another, they drove the herds through the lake to remove ticks from their thick wool.

Chances are these remedies and the buckaroo story were inspired by similar tales told by Indians who came to the lake during their annual hunting and gathering trips. The Indians called Soap Lake "Smokiam," meaning "healing waters" or "medicine lake," and declared it a place where

Soap Lake. The white stripe along the shoreline is the flakes that feel like soap–the origin of the lake's name.

no wars would be fought. Long before any white man discovered the lake, tribes from as far away as the Great Plains came there to gather camas roots, race horses, trade goods, and heal their sick in the stream huts they built along the shoreline. Even the healthy would use the huts to cleanse their bodies of disease-causing impurities. The cowboys were probably the first people to change the lake's name to Soap Lake after the frothy, soapy bubbles the breezes whipped up along the shoreline.

Lucy B. Gray became the first white settler to homestead on the lakeshore when she chose a parcel on the southwestern corner of the lake in 1903. A year later, Carl Jensen opened the first store on the south shore of the lake, and the town of Soap Lake was born. The Siloam Hotel, the first sanitarium, was built in 1906 and expanded quickly as people came from around the world to heal their rheumatism, circulatory disorders, and skin conditions by soaking in the mineral waters and taking mud baths.

Within three years, the hotel grew from 30 rooms to 45 on 420 acres with lake frontage. Even with the extra rooms and three new hotels nearby, there was not enough space to accommodate all the guests, so the owners set up overflow tents behind their hotels. An early resident whose parents owned one of the hotels said he remembered coming home often on summer evenings and discovering his bedroom had been rented.

To reach Soap Lake, travelers took one of the four daily trains to Ephrata, six miles west of Soap Lake, or Adrian, five miles east of Soap Lake, and hire a ride the rest of the way. A hack and driver from each sanitarium met every train. Most people came without reservations and were too sick to protest when the strongest or fastest driver shanghaied them. Competition was so fierce, the drivers often brawled until the sheriff broke them up. Finally, the Northern Pacific Railroad set up a special parking lot and a rotating system to give each hotel a turn to pick up its passengers. The ride shortened in 1911, when a new station opened at Grand Orchards, two miles from Soap Lake.

By the time the town was officially incorporated in 1919, Soap Lake had an atmosphere and reputation similar to New Orleans. Four resort hotels, rooming houses and apartments, and businesses catering to campers by renting tents, boats, and bathing suits boomed. Hotel guests often regained their health in time to seek entertainment, and residents of the sparsely populated country were always "hot just to get to be with someone," according to one old-timer. It was almost impossible to walk down the main street on summer nights because of the crowds on the sidewalks. Restaurants, saloons, and the weekly dances at the Siloam Hotel were attended well.

With continued growth came new problems. Battles started between men over their desire to court the same woman. One dispute ended when a jilted lover stood on Main Street and blasted a rival's house with a shotgun. Fortunately, his target dodged the pellets, which flew through the front wall and out the back, but a doctor had to treat him for wounds inflicted by flying splinters.

Guns were finally outlawed in town because fun-seekers would sit on the shore of Soap Lake and take pot shots at low-flying birds, narrowly missing swimmers. Swimming in the lake without bathing suits caused an uproar with the prominent townsfolk, so local newspapers reminded swimmers to dress appropriately. Cowboys and city officials locked horns over the main street, the same route used for the cattle drives. City officials did not believe herding cattle through the center of town created a good impression for the tourists and asked the cowboys to move the trail. The cowboys refused, so the town built a stockade, impounded stray animals, and charged a dollar a head for their release. The cowboys retaliated by sneaking into town one night and destroying the corral. After the townspeople rebuilt it, the cowboys destroyed it again. That happened several times before the cowboys decided to move the trail. None of my sources explain why the cowboys changed their minds or whether any were arrested for vandalism.

The town also attracted the area's only con artist, E. Paul Janes. From 1907 through 1915, Janes operated real estate and insurance offices in Soap Lake, Ephrata, and Seattle. Janes or one of his colleagues met Easterners unfamiliar with the area at local railroad depots in the surrounding area and showed them a prime piece of farmland near Soap Lake. Then he sold the property to them at prices ranging from $250 to $1,500. When the buyers tried to settle there, they learned they actually bought an arid, non-productive rocky parcel a short distance away.

Janes also sold stock in several business ventures that never materialized, such as making a vapor-bath cabinet designed for using

A marker for the Cariboo Trail, one of the main cattle drive routes through central Washington to the British Columbia interior.

Soap Lake water and manufacturing salts and other products made from the lake's water. From 1911 through 1916, dissatisfied investors sued him six times in Grant County, but all the cases were settled out of court. His exploits ended when he traveled to New York City to buy some machinery for his salts manufacturing plant, and one of his associates in Soap Lake sent him an urgent telegram. He suddenly took a vacation in Europe and never returned.

Soap Lake's popularity as a health resort declined in the 1920s after fire destroyed the four hotels. The Great Depression and a drought in 1933 caused many farmers to declare bankruptcy and more businesses to close or leave. Finally, World War II intervened in any plans to rebuild.

Today, however, Soap Lake is once again attracting people seeking cures for their ailments. Some of the local hotels pump water from the lake into guests' bathrooms, and the staff recommends soaking in it to feel rejuvenated. Memories of Soap Lake's heyday live on in local museums and the sections of the cattle trail are still visible from State Highway 17 north of town.

Misadventures at Battle Rock

Port Orford, Oregon

Among the many Old West conflicts between the whites and the Indians, one of the most unusual was the war between nine pioneers and an estimated 300 Indian braves at Battle Rock, near what is now known as the town of Port Orford on the southern Oregon Coast.

William Tichenor, the captain of the *Sea Gull,* traveled often along the coastline from Portland to San Francisco during the 1840s and 1850s. The area around Port Orford (known in those days as Fort Orford) caught his attention as he envisioned a profitable venture. Because he believed this small harbor was near the inland trails of the Willamette and Rogue River Valleys, he decided it would be a good place to build a trading post and road leading to the gold diggings in southern Oregon.

On one of his trips to Portland in late May 1851, Tichenor met James Kirkpatrick, a carpenter, and convinced him to lead an expedition to Fort Orford to start the project. Anyone who helped, including Kirkpatrick, would receive shares of the land in exchange for their efforts. Tichenor claimed the Indians at Fort Orford were friendly, although it appears he never contacted any of them to find out.

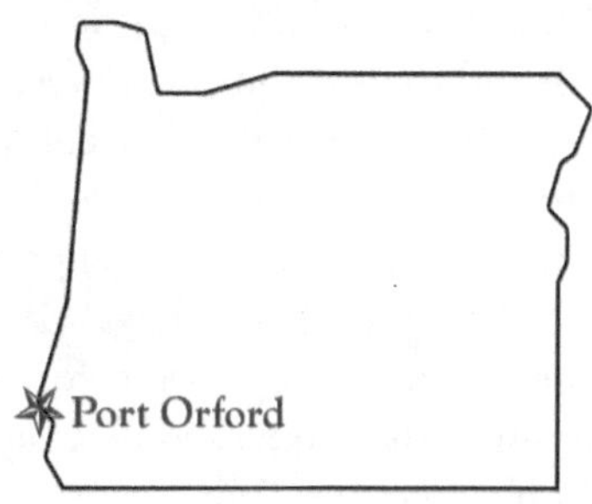

Kirkpatrick found eight men to accompany him on the trip—J.H. Eagen, John T. Slater, George Ridoubs, T.D. Palmer, Joseph Hussey, Cyrus W. Hedden, James Carigan, and Erastus Summers.

Tichenor offered them ammunition, supplies, and a ride on the *Sea Gull to* San Francisco. They left Portland on June 4, 1851.

During a layover in Astoria, Kirkpatrick and his men grew wary about Tichenor's assurance about friendly Indians living at the new settlement site. To relieve their fears, Kirkpatrick asked Tichenor what types of weapons were being supplied.

"Oh, there is no danger from the Indians," the overconfident captain replied. But Kirkpatrick and his men refused to go any farther until Tichenor found adequate arms. The captain bought three old flintlock muskets; one old sword, half-eaten with rust; a few pounds of lead; and three or four pounds of powder at a junk shop.

Obviously, the men weren't satisfied with Tichenor's choices of protection and voiced their opinions. "You will never need them," Tichenor said, "but having them will make you look dangerous anyway."

Kirkpatrick decided to find weapons for his group. He left the ship and met a young officer from Fort George, who sold him an Army rifle and some ammunition for $20. This purchase, along with a rifle, a .38-caliber shooting revolver, and a pair of derringers the men brought from Portland, increased their feelings of security.

Four days later, the *Sea Gull* arrived at Fort Orford, and Kirkpatrick and his men didn't like what they saw. According to accounts written by this expedition leader, "There were a few Indians in sight who appeared friendly, but I could see that they did not like to have us there."

This observation prompted the party to demand that a small cannon, stored on the steamer, be sent with them before they would go ashore. Tichenor finally gave it to them, while wondering what the fuss was about, and said he would return in 15 days.

After unloading the supplies, the men immediately set up camp on Battle Rock, a long, narrow ridge of stone extending from Fort Orford toward the Pacific Ocean. The rock was surrounded on three sides by water; the other connected the beach. At high tide, the sea surrounded the entire rock. The party's camp was located halfway up the rock on a narrow, level patch of ground facing the beach.

Kirkpatrick and Eagen loaded the cannon and aimed it toward the beach in preparation for the fight they thought was likely. The ammunition consisted of a variety of items, as Kirkpatrick describes in his account: "We put in a two pound sack of powder and on top of that about half a cotton shirt and then on top of that as much bar lead cut up in pieces of from one to two inches in length as I could hold in my hands, and then a couple of old newspapers on top. We then primed the gun with some fine rifle powder and trained it so as to rake the narrow ridge in front of the muzzle, and the gun was ready for use."

As soon as the Indians saw the steamer leave, Kirkpatrick said, "They appeared very cross and ordered us away, making signs to us that they would kill us if we did not go. Then they left for their camps down the beach."

This hadn't been the first time the Indians saw white men. According to Susan Ned, a Coquille, her ancestors saw them sail past their camps much earlier. Often they stopped and traded with her ancestors. In the 1830s, according to legends, a Russian ship wrecked near Coos Bay. Some of the sailors married Indian women and settled on the south coast.

The Coquilles believed one of these sailors, known by his red shirt, was rescued from that shipwreck by Indians from another tribe. Later, he lived with one of the tribes at Fort Orford. This man might have convinced the Indians to fight Kirkpatrick's party. By this time,

Battle Rock, the site of the skirmish between Kirkpatrick's party and the Coquille Indians near Port Orford..

the Indians were determined to defend their land from any threats of takeover by the white men. Also, the Indians were not pleased when Kirkpatrick and his party refused to trade with them.

Early the next day, the Indians had a war dance. According to Kirkpatrick, when they finished, they "started shooting arrows at us from too great a distance to do any damage." Then, "about 9 o'clock a large canoe, containing twelve warriors, came up the coast from the direction of the mouth of the Rogue River. Among them was one tall fellow wearing a red shirt who seemed to be their leader. As soon as the canoe touched the sand, they all jumped out and carried it onto the beach. The fellow in the red shirt drew a long knife, waved it over his head, gave a terrible yell and, with at least one hundred of his soldiers, started for us with a rush. I stood by the gun holding a piece of tarred rope with one end in the fire ready, as soon as the Indians crowded on the narrow ridge in front of the cannon, to let them have the contents when it would do the most damage."

When the warriors and their leader were in range, Kirkpatrick fired. The Indians had never seen a gun like this one, and the noise frightened them. Some fled, but others stayed, and whenever one moved too close, Kirkpatrick's men would shoot.

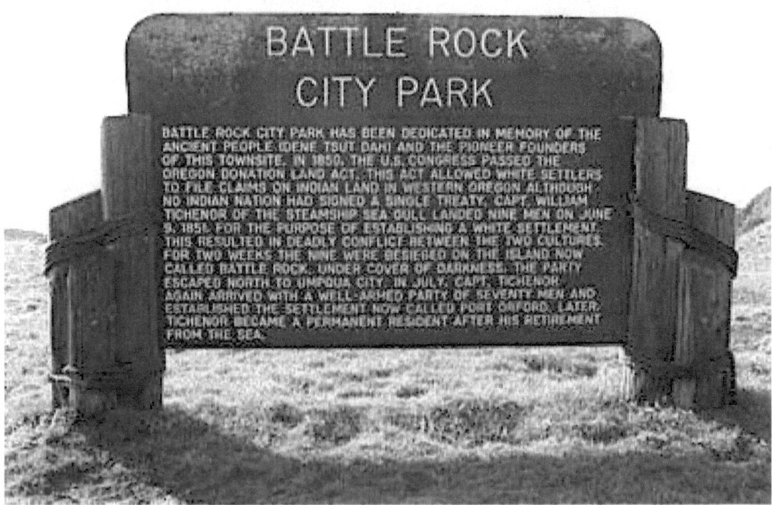

A marker at Battle Rock near Port Orford, Oregon, describing the conflict between Kirkpatrick's party and the Coquille Indians.

By the time the battle ended, 23 Indians were dead and two of the small party were wounded. The Indians retreated, and the chief sent an emissary to ask permission to carry away the dead. Kirkpatrick gave permission and said another Indian could help. He also told the chief they would break camp when the *Sea Gull* returned 14 days later.

The two Indians removed all the bodies, except the red-shirted man. When Kirkpatrick asked the chief about this, he became angry, muttered a few words Kirkpatrick couldn't understand, tore off the dead man's shirt, kicked him, and left the body on the beach.

The Indians expected the men to keep their promise about leaving. On the morning of the fifteenth day, about 300 to 400 braves appeared on the beach in war paint. Kirkpatrick tried to explain he was only waiting for the ship, but the Indians no longer trusted him. They started a war dance, and each time they turned to face the rock, "they would snap their bow strings at us and make signs that they would soon have our scalps," Kirkpatrick said.

At the time, Kirkpatrick and his party didn't know the *Sea Gull* had been embargoed for debt in San Francisco. Colonel John B. Ferguson, U.S. mail agent for California and Oregon and a friend of Kirkpatrick, heard about Tichenor's problem. Knowing the nature of the Indians on the southern Oregon Coast, Ferguson realized Kirkpatrick and his men were in trouble. Ferguson asked the captain of the *Columbia* to return to Portland one day earlier than scheduled, with Tichenor on board, and gave strict orders to stop at Fort Orford to rescue Kirkpatrick's party.

Meanwhile, at the site of the siege, the chief gathered nearly 300 warriors about 250 yards from the white men's camp, gave a speech, and charged. When they were in shooting range, Kirkpatrick and Carigan fired at the chief, killing him instantly. The Indians removed his body and retreated for about an hour. Then they charged again. The besieged whites killed their new leader, which caused another retreat.

The Indians held a meeting about 300 yards from Battle Rock, "after which they commenced going down the beach to a place over a mile from our camp, where there were a number of fires burning," Kirkpatrick later said. "We could see a number of canoes loaded with Indians coming up from the direction of the north of the Rogue River and landing near these fires. They were evidently concentrating their forces for a night attack on us."

Kirkpatrick knew if his party were attacked at night, they wouldn't have a chance. He suggested they try to escape.

Kirkpatrick wrote a note, which he placed in the back of an old book and buried it about a foot deep at the stump of a pine tree. His note read, "We are now surrounded by three or four hundred Indians hungry for scalps, on one side, by thousands of miles of water on the other, and at least 150 miles away from any white man's house. We have but little grub and are nearly out of ammunition and if the Indians should make a night attack or rush on us we certainly could not defend ourselves against so many." He included the accounts he wrote of both battles with this note.

The men crept from Battle Rock unseen, but on the beach, 30 Indians spotted them and started chasing them. The men lost the braves in the timber and brush of the mountains nearby. For two and a half days, the men traveled almost continuously, alternating between forest and beach until reaching the Coquille River.

On the other side of the river, they saw two Coquille Indian villages. Despite their apparent danger, they made a temporary camp on a ridge nearby and built a fire to keep warm.

The next day, Indians from the village advanced on the men. They escaped through the woods to Whiskey Run, a beach 27 miles north of Battle Rock. A friendly Indian who claimed to have seen Kirkpatrick in Portland followed them there and warned him that the Coquilles were still in pursuit. This Indian led the men to a white pole standing in a huge pile of rocks at the edge of the beach. When they passed the pole, which marked the end of Coquille territory, the Indian said the men were safe. If the Coquilles went any farther, the Coos, Umpqua, Klickitat, and other tribes to the north could drive them back.

The men camped in a small cove for the night and continued to Coos Bay the following day. There, they met the Coos Indians, who, according to Kirkpatrick, were very hospitable. "The Indians met us more than a mile from camp and brought us dried salmon, dried elk meat and salmon berries," he said. "We stayed all night with these Indians who seemed to vie with each other in doing everything they could for us. In the morning they took us across the bay and landed us about where Empire City now stands. They told us that we would make the mouth of the Umpqua the next day."

About 24 hours later, Kirkpatrick's party finally found refuge at Umpqua City, a new settlement established by a land company at the mouth of the Umpqua River. Their suspenseful journey from Fort Orford had lasted eight days.

Ironically, the *Columbia* arrived at Fort Orford one day after Kirkpatrick and his party escaped. The captain and several passengers came ashore and found the body of the red-shirted man and the note. After a search revealed some human teeth and charred pieces of human bones in the ashes of an old Indian bonfire, they assumed the men had been massacred and burned.

The word spread to Portland, and the local newspapers quickly printed the story. It was quite a surprise when Kirkpatrick returned to Portland a month later and said every white man survived the attack.

Today, Battle Rock is a park, a popular stop for tourists. A marker overlooking this former battleground summarizes the story of this small party's struggle against impossible odds. The park is south of downtown Port Orford on U.S. Highway 101.

Mother-Daughter Heroines of the Rogue Indian War

Grants Pass, Oregon

The early 1850s was a stormy time for the pioneers in the Rogue River Valley of southwestern Oregon. As more people moved in from the East, tensions rose between the settlers and the Indians who had occupied the land for hundreds of years. The rising pressures finally erupted into the Rogue Indian War from October 1855 to June 1856.

One of the boldest defenses by the pioneers in the valley occurred on October 9, 1855. The Rogue River tribes were raiding as many homes as possible near present-day Grants Pass. After killing Mrs. J. Wagner and Mary, her four-year-old daughter, the Indians moved toward the home of George and Mary Ann Harris.

As soon as George saw the Indians preparing to strike, he ran into the cabin and grabbed his gun. Accounts on what happened next vary. In one version, George shot one Indian and wounded another while the group of about 21 braves shouted and made violent displays. In another version, he was shot and mortally wounded while closing the door of the family's cabin. In both versions of the story, the shot killed him.

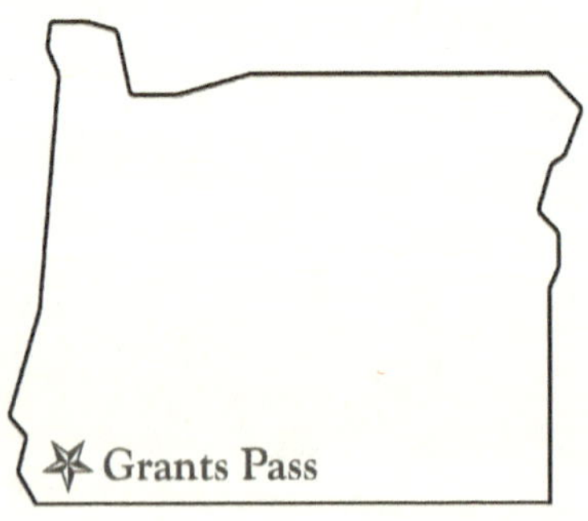

Sophie, George and Mary Ann's teenage daughter, was injured by the gunfire. In one version of the story, she ran outside when her father was shot and was hit with a bullet in her right arm, between her shoulder and elbow. In another account, she was struck between her elbow and wrist when a musket ball flew through a muslin-covered window of the cabin and broke her bone.

When George was shot, he told Mary Ann to bar the doors and load the guns. Mary Ann didn't know how to load a gun, but George managed to show her how to do it before he died.

Mary Ann drug her husband inside the cabin and barred the door. While standing guard, she showed Sophie how to load the guns. Then she moved around the cabin, shooting through the cracks to try to convince the Indians that several people were inside. By then, the braves had burned all the outbuildings and were trying to set the cabin on fire. Sophie continued loading the guns for her mother, despite her injuries.

Late that afternoon, the braves withdrew when they heard shots about a mile away. Fearing they would return, Mary Ann and Sophie fled the cabin and hid under a pile of brush nearby. The Indians returned, discovered the home abandoned, and started to raid it. Mary Ann fired and scared them away. This back-and-forth continued until the Indians surrounded Mary Ann and Sophia. They didn't want to kill women and children; they wanted to capture the pair. Mary Ann continued firing to keep them at a distance.

The next morning, a militia commanded by Major Fitzgerald arrived and scared the Indians away. They found Mary Ann blackened with powder and stained with blood and Sophie in pain. The troops took Mary Ann and Sophie to Jacksonville, where a prominent businessman and trustee, John Love, took them in. In exchange for room and board, Mary Ann cared for John's ailing mother until her death. Sophie married John one year later.

There are two versions of the story about what happened to the Harris family's cabin. In one version, volunteers from Jacksonville returned to the homestead and buried George below the cabin floor. They burned the cabin to hide any evidence of his grave. A few years after the war, George's body was moved to the Jacksonville Cemetery, where it rests today. In the other version, the Indians burned the cabin after the militia took Mary Ann and Sophie to Jacksonville. This version does not provide any details about what happened to George's body.

On Valentine's Day 1863, Mary Ann married Aaron Chambers, and they lived in Jacksonville. She died there on February 17, 1882, as a highly respected woman of the community. She was buried in the Jacksonville Cemetery.

The Rogue River.

Noah Kellogg's Silver Mountain

Kellogg, Idaho

Bad luck followed Noah Kellogg everywhere. For years, he had been a nomadic jack-of-all-trades who failed at almost everything he tried. But the quiet, curious roamer didn't give up easily, and his persistence eventually paid off with one of the richest silver mines in the West.

Noah's wanderings began shortly after his marriage to a Mrs. Byrd, who worked as a matron in the psychiatric hospital in Steilacoom, Washington Territory. He was an attendant at the same institution in 1873, a bachelor of nearly 50 years old when the couple decided to tie the knot.

They lived briefly in Tacoma, Washington; Nanaimo and Victoria, British Columbia; and Portland, Oregon. Noah worked at odd jobs cutting timber, clearing rights-of-way, digging ditches, and managing a saloon. The damp climate provided little comfort for Noah's rheumatism and Mrs. Kellogg's severe asthma, so they moved to Dayton, where the drier air of eastern Washington provided relief.

Noah borrowed money to build a small house of undressed lumber. He also used some of the funds to buy four yokes of oxen to haul logs from the Blue Mountains in eastern Oregon to a small sawmill in Dayton. One day, he received word that his wife had suffered a stroke, so he hurried home to be with her. His businesses had been growing, but his prolonged stay at home caused him to lose his oxen.

Noah realized if he didn't find work soon, he would lose his home. In 1875, he reluctantly left his wife with one of his stepdaughters, who agreed to care for her.

For seven years, he traveled throughout the West, often ill and unemployed. He was in California when news broke of gold discoveries in the Coeur d'Alene Mountains. In 1882, Andrew J. Pritchard found gold in the sands of Eagle, Beaver, and Pritchard Creeks, prompting a rush to the Idaho Panhandle. As Noah lay on his cot in a miner's cabin, he had a vision of a huge mountain, filled with gold and silver, waiting for him somewhere. If only he could get to Idaho, he believed, he might find it.

When he arrived in Eagle City in May 1884, Noah was down to his last $5. A man lent him $16, and Noah moved on to Murray, where he bought a whipsaw and began cutting lumber for miners. His venture failed, however, when another man opened a water-powered sawmill.

Ditch digging and carpentry helped pay Noah's bills temporarily while he looked for other opportunities. Soon he opened a shingle mill, but when the mill started, the knives he made from a used saw blade flew to pieces. He was $300 in debt and never sold a shingle.

As a last resort, Noah turned to the mountains in pursuit of his vision, but before he could prospect, he needed financial support. In August 1885, he asked for help from O.O. Peck, a small-time contractor for whom Noah worked briefly. Peck did not want to risk money on the unlikely proposal, but when Noah pressed him, he contacted Dr. J.T. Cooper, a former surgeon in the British Navy. Cooper also declined.

Noah changed his strategy when he saw Peck's and Cooper's irritation over a loud, braying burro that frequently kept the residents of Murray awake at night. "Put a grubstake on that jackass' back and I'll take him out in the hills where he can't bother you," Noah said. The offer was too good to refuse. Cooper and Peck took Noah to Jim Wardner's store and charged $17 worth of provisions: 35 pounds of bacon, 10 pounds of beans, 15 pounds of flour, and small quantities of coffee and sugar.

The burro cost another $3. A miner from Colorado abandoned the animal at Murray, but someone suddenly claimed ownership.

Noah loaded the pack on the burro and started his adventure.

Kellogg, Idaho.

Sources conflict about what happened next. Most say Noah didn't know the burro often strayed. It managed to wander up Milo Gulch on the South Fork of the Coeur d'Alene River. When he finally found it, he noticed the independent animal had stumbled upon one of the richest ledges of galena (a mixture of silver and lead) in the world.

Another version of the story, which Noah told to Judge John R. McBride, differed considerably. Noah claimed the burro had been trained to follow him "like a puppy." The day Noah discovered the galena, the burro became stubborn and refused to move. Noah grabbed its halter and unsuccessfully tried to lead it. Even when he tried to drive the animal, it held its ground.

Noah's patience turned to anger. He slapped the burro's rump with a willow switch. It leapt forward a couple of paces and stopped across the trail, pointed its head toward a distant peak, and brayed.

Remembering Numbers 22:28, Noah decided the burro might be trying to tell him something: "The Lord opened the donkey's mouth, and it said to Balaam, 'What have I done to you that you have beaten me these three times?'" Balaam's donkey refused to move, because it saw an angel barring the way with a sword, which Balaam could not see.

When Noah reached the mountain the burro pointed to, he found it was almost solid galena. He immediately staked two claims, giving himself one-half interest in both and Cooper and Peck one-fourth each. Quickly he grabbed some samples and rushed back to Murray. In his haste, he forgot the burro.

At the mining camp, he found Dr. Cooper, showed him the ore, and asked for a meal because he hadn't eaten all day. Cooper wasn't impressed with the galena and virtually threw Noah out the door.

Noah might have been eager to show off his find because instead of finding Peck, he went to the saloon and gambling hall Jacob "Dutch Jake" Goetz operated. Goetz recognized the value of the samples, set up a delicious, hearty meal for Kellogg, and tracked down Phil O'Rourke, who knew more about ore than he did. O'Rourke was also excited when he saw the samples.

Dutch Jake bought supplies and provided horses, and Noah, O'Rourke, and another miner named Con Sullivan went to the mountain and posted claims on both sides of Milo Gulch. The two original claims Noah staked were named the Bunker Hill and the Sullivan, and they became two of the largest producers of silver in the world.

The find also prompted one of the largest mining lawsuits in history. Cooper and Peck claimed they first heard about the find several days after Noah, O'Rourke, and Sullivan posted claims. The two backers became angry and hired lawyer Major W.W. Woods to represent them in court.

Major Woods insisted that Noah thought he shouldn't share his newfound fortune with such stingy backers. Therefore, when he returned to Murray, he went straight to Goetz and O'Rourke, trying to cheat Cooper and Peck of their legal shares.

William T. Stoll, the plaintiffs' junior counsel, and a young prospector named John Flaherty conducted an investigation at Milo Gulch. There Flaherty found a crumpled piece of paper with the inscription, "N.S. Kellogg, 1/2; J.T. Cooper, 1/4; O.O. Peck, 1/4, locators." Stoll believed the evidence proved that Noah posted claims in his own name and his original partners' names, then discarded the notices and substituted his, O'Rourke's, and Sullivan's names on new postings.

The burro entered the case, too. When Noah returned to the claims with his new partners, he picked up the burro along the trail. Some accounts indicate the judge considered the animal's presence while making his decision. The burro was declared a co-discoverer, and because it belonged to Cooper and Peck, they were entitled to profit by that fact.

The case went to trial in June 1886 before Territorial District Judge Normal Buck in the rude little courthouse at Murray, then the Shoshone County seat. The benches outside the rail overflowed with interested miners favoring Noah, O'Rourke, and Sullivan.

W.H. Clagett, one of the defense attorneys, requested a jury, although the judge was expected to make the final decision in equity cases. Clagett assured the judge he did not question the judge's fairness and ability. Instead, Clagett argued a jury could help unscramble the complicated case. Judge Buck allowed the motion.

During Noah's testimony, Major Woods led him into some dangerous admissions. One was that Noah couldn't have been starving when he returned to Murray. He was gone only three days, and one man could not consume such a large grubstake so soon. Then Noah was asked to write his name several times. His signature matched the one on the crumpled claim notice.

The jury deliberated only a few minutes before deciding against Peck and Cooper. But a few days later, Judge Buck delivered an opposing decision, which was upheld as a case of clear fraud.

The losers filed a notice of appeal, but while the case was pending in the U.S. Supreme Court, Simeon G. Reed, a Portland financier, offered to buy the mine for $1.5 million. His only stipulation was that the title be clear.

All parties quickly agreed to compromise instead of losing a chance at wealth. They drew up an agreement giving Noah $300,000, O'Rourke $200,000, Cooper and Peck $76,000 each, and Sullivan $75,000. Several others involved in the case received lesser sums. Cooper and Peck profited greatly in their investment, considering that they paid only $2.40 toward the $17 bill for Noah's supplies. Although Jim Wardner never received the remaining balance, he made a tidy sum from the settlement. He had the foresight to file for water rights in the stream above the Bunker Hill and Sullivan mines, which he sold to the new owners. In addition, he got a contract for extracting ore.

The discovery of the Bunker Hill and Sullivan lodes brought hundreds of prospectors to northern Idaho. Brothers Robert and Jonathan Ingalls laid out a town and called it Milo, after the creek that ran down Milo Gulch. The name was later changed to Kellogg, in honor of Noah. Other good finds followed, and several mines went into production. By 1889, the Coeur d'Alene region was producing approximately $2.5 million in metals, primarily silver and lead. Production doubled a year later.

Noah planned to stay in Kellogg until he received the first payment from the sale of the claims, then return to his wife in Dayton. Then he received a letter from the stepdaughter who cared for his wife. Mrs. Kellogg died in July 1886, almost a year after he made his lucky strike.

The daughter read about Noah's connection with the mine in the newspapers. She wrote about her struggles to care for her mother and her hopes that Noah would return. Widowed and destitute, she asked Noah to come and help her.

Noah immediately got a $1,000 advance and left to find his stepdaughter and learn more about his wife's long illness and death. When the sale was completed, Noah spent thousands of dollars on his wife's children. Soon their demands became exorbitant, so he refused to make any more payments.

The daughter who remained with Mrs. Kellogg sued the new mine owners. According to the common-property laws of Idaho, if a husband abandons his wife, her entire estate should go to the children upon her death. Because Noah abandoned his wife, the stepdaughter asserted, the children were entitled to her share of the mine. The court found no proof that Noah abandoned his wife, and under the law, he had a right to sell the property.

After the trial, Noah retired to Kellogg and enjoyed his status as a respected citizen and namesake of the town. He died March 17, 1903. His grave is in Greenwood Cemetery on a knoll overlooking the mountain where the stubborn burro helped him find his vision.

The burro's fate remains unknown. According to one account, the animal became a privileged character around Murray, but its bray kept people awake and the miners eventually forgot about the burro's contribution to their well-being. One night, they lashed several sticks of dynamite to the burro's body, added a long fuse, and prodded it toward the outskirts of town. As it ran one way, the miners hurried it in the opposite direction. The other account indicates the burro was pampered for the rest of its life at an Oregon farm.

Today, the town of Kellogg is a quiet place, where mining continues on a smaller scale. Silver was the town's lifeblood until the early 1980s, after the metal rose to its highest price ever, then fell sharply. An abrupt collapse of the local economy followed the mine closures in 1981.

In 1985, the city council started planning to build a gondola to the top of Kellogg Peak, the site of the old Silverhorn ski area in the Bitterroot Mountains. The result was Silver Mountain Resort, which opened in 1990 and attracts skiers from around the world. Crystal Gold Mine, a working gold mine during the 1880s, is open daily. Visitors can view exhibits at the museum and take a guided tour of the mine.

Along the mountains surrounding Kellogg and its sister city, Wardner, scars from silver mining are visible. They're remnants of the great industry that started when Noah Kellogg and his burro discovered galena more than a century earlier.

The base of Silver Mountain Resort in Kellogg, Idaho.

The Beef Between the Songhees and the British

Victoria, British Columbia

On March 13, 1843, Hudson's Bay Company Chief Factor James Douglas, accompanied by 15 men, boarded the steamer *Beaver* at Fort Nisqually, Washington. After a brief stop near Dungeness Spit for fresh fish, they crossed the Strait of Juan de Fuca and anchored off Vancouver Island at Shoal Point in Victoria Harbor. The *Beaver* landed at Clover Point the next morning, and Douglas and his men walked along the shore to Beacon Hill before crossing to the Inner Harbor, where they began building Fort Victoria.

Three days later, Douglas discussed his intentions to establish a fort at Inner Harbor with the native Samose (Songhee) Indians. The Songhees seemed pleased and even offered to help with the construction. For every 40 pickets they provided to Douglas, he paid them with a blanket.

The Indians and new British settlers lived in harmony. A year after the British arrived, the Songhees moved closer to the fort along the shores of Inner Harbor. The fort stood between present-day View and Broughton Streets below Government Street, and the village sprouted along the edge of the woods by the banks of a gorge where Johnson Street is today.

Unfortunately, the peaceful coexistence did not last. One of the British discovered the

The Parliament Building in Victoria. The land surrounding this building was the site of the Songhee-British dispute.

Songhees killed some of their oxen feeding in the open spaces near the fort. When Roderick Finlayson, who was considered the official founder of Victoria, demanded payment from a Songhee chief, the man "went away in a rage, assembled some Cowichan Indians to his village and the next move I found on their part was a shower of bullets fired at the fort, with a great noise and demonstration on the part of the crowd assembled, threatening death and devastation to all the white," Finlayson wrote in his unpublished autobiography.

After creating a ruse to ensure an Indian lodge was empty, Finlayson fired a nine-pounder loaded with grapeshot into the building. Because the lodge was built of poles and cedar boards, the ammunition "flew into the air in splinters like a bombshell, after this there was such howling that I thought a number were killed," Finlayson wrote.

Fortunately, no one was killed or injured, but the Songhees were frightened after the demonstration, according to an interpreter who stopped by the fort later. They weren't aware of the power of the British weapons.

Shortly afterward, Finlayson convinced the Songhee chief that the Hudson's Bay Company would level the village and drive the Indians out of the harbor if they did not pay for the slaughtered oxen immediately. The chief paid Finlayson a day later.

There weren't any more conflicts between the British and Songhees. The people at the fort talked about what happened long after the dispute ended.

The Curse of Monte Cristo

Monte Cristo, Washington

Nature has fought the mining town of Monte Cristo, Washington, from its birth.

On July 3, 1889, a treacherous mountain storm forced prospectors Frank Peabody and Joseph Pearsall, who were following the north branch of the Skykomish River from Index, Washington, into the Cascade Mountains, to take cover for the night. The next day, they emerged from the storm-tossed forest near the top of Silver Top Mountain and saw a red-gold ledge running up the side of another mountain across the valley. After studying the ledge through field glasses, Peabody proclaimed, "There's enough gold in that mountain to make the Count of Monte Cristo look like a pauper." The town of Monte Cristo grew from this discovery, but throughout its short life, the same kind of rough weather that hit the prospectors plagued the community.

Pearsall and Peabody realized the usual assortment of inexpensive prospecting tools wouldn't budge the giant lode, so they sought advice and financial help in Seattle. Peabody found an old acquaintance, John McDonald "Mac" Wilmans. Mac and his brother, Fred, successfully invested in real estate, mining stock, and railroads in other western boom towns. After studying the prospectors' ore samples, Mac returned to the mountain with Pearsall

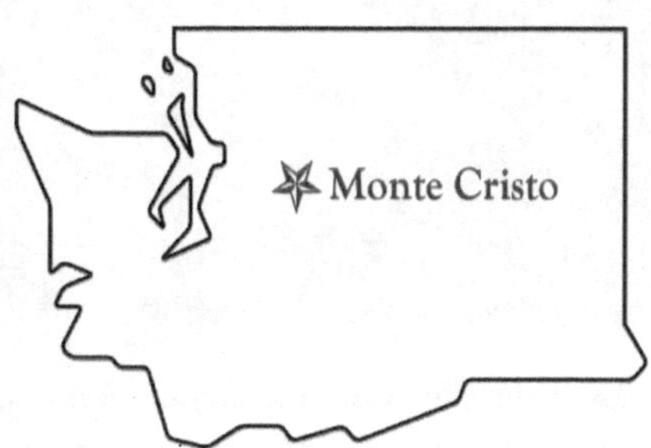

and Peabody. When he saw the amazing site, he wired Fred with a proposal to grubstake the two prospectors. Fred agreed. While Pearsall and Peabody located claims, the Wilmanses gathered more investors.

They finished all arrangements by the end of April 1890. The Wilmanses and their hired hands began moving equipment toward the proposed camp, but nature protested. Snow blocked the party's way 12 miles from their destination, so they stopped to wait for the weather to improve. Because of the delay, it took two months to

Even the ghosts are friendly in Monte Cristo! This sign welcoming hikers to the town leans against a tree at the entrance to the abandoned site.

Monte Cristo, Washington.

move in all the supplies and mining equipment.

Within a few months, a foot trail connected the camp to the outside world. Miners built a 15-foot-square log cabin with a stone fireplace, known as "the '76 Cabin," on the high bank of '76 Creek.

As the word spread about the new camp, more people moved to the area and established the town of Monte Cristo in 1891. Until the Everett and Monte Cristo Railway arrived in 1893, pack trains, wagons, and stages delivered supplies and provisions.

By 1894, Monte Cristo was thriving. Population estimates ranged from 1,000 to 2,000. Prospectors and speculators staked hundreds of claims. Aerial tramways carried ore from the mines to a 200-ton concentrator near town. The railroad hauled two carloads of ore daily to a smelter established in the lumber town of Everett in 1891 for Monte Cristo ore.

During the boom years, Monte Cristo had a post office, mercantile store, hotel, money order office, volunteer fire department, sawmill, and newspaper, the *Monte Cristo Mountaineer*. The town attempted to build a jail, but on the night of June 28, 1891, someone tore it down and tossed it in the river. No records indicate whether the vandals were found, and no one attempted to rebuild the jail.

Throughout the 1890s and early 1900s, Monte Cristo's life revolved around the success of the mines in the district. The Pride, Mystery, and Justice were three of the best, shipping ores valued at over $2.5 million. Many eastern capitalists, including John D. Rockefeller, became interested in the district and invested heavily in its operations.

Like all western mining towns, Monte Cristo had its share of wild times. The shanties in the slum district attracted a lot of attention. Shootings and knifings were frequent. Tempers occasionally flared at the Blazing Stump—a combination saloon, dance hall, gambling den, and brothel—but as long as the fighters killed one another, the townspeople shrugged it off. When an innocent bystander fell victim, however, they became angry because the town had no sheriff or deputy to keep the peace.

Despite Monte Cristo's growth, nature continued fighting against the town. Just before winter arrived (winter could linger from November to May), residents moved the pack animals out of the valley. But the roads around the plant and terminal stations had to be kept open, and without the animals, this was a grueling task. Heavy snows forced the railroad to use its snowplows constantly and avalanches destroyed tramways and cabins. In the spring, fierce rains caused mudslides, which washed out the wagon road and railroad. Rock slides in the summer were just as destructive.

In the fall of 1897, a flood wiped out the railroad. Rockefeller rebuilt it and continued large-scale mining until 1903, when he sold his interests. Ten years later, mining resumed on a smaller scale, and hopes were high that another boom would take place.

"There is a stir and bustle in Monte Cristo that reminds mining men of the early days, when the Rockefeller interests operated on an extensive scale, taking out silver and its by-product, arsenic," the *Seattle Post-Intelligencer* reported. As of July 30, 1913, 75 men were working in five mining camps, and owners planned to make shipments early in September.

Success was short-lived, however. Bad weather hampered operations and made the work too costly. By 1917, Monte Cristo was a ghost town. The longer the town was abandoned, the more heavy snows and vandals damaged the empty buildings.

Several entrepreneurs tried to transform Monte Cristo into a resort town. Tourism surged after World War II and peaked in

1980, when a flood destroyed the gravel road owned by the county. The county decided against repairing the road, so the resort closed. The lodge burned to the ground in March 1983 under suspicious circumstances.

A month later, the Monte Cristo Preservation Association was formed to protect and restore the site. Today, Monte Cristo has a collection of cabins surrounded by the Henry M. Jackson Wilderness. The ghost town attracts summer hikers and curious sightseers, who walk four miles along an old gravel and dirt road to view the remains.

Gold fever is still alive, and some developers are trying to bring mining back to the district. A 1983 U.S. Bureau of Mines report estimated the area may hold more than 50 million tons of ore containing gold, silver, copper, lead, and zinc—mostly on private land. But the report also warned the climate and topography create "unusually severe mining problems." Apparently, nature still controls Monte Cristo's fate.

The Curtis Sheep Massacre

Okanogan Valley, Washington

By the end of the nineteenth century, cattle ranching thrived in the Okanogan Valley in northcentral Washington. Pioneers who settled there pastured cattle on open range owned by the United States government and relied on livestock sales as their sole income.

Soon sheep ranches threatened the ample food supplies on the range. Cattle will not graze on land that sheep have grazed heavily, because sheep generally pull grass by the roots, reducing the amount of available pasture. This destruction angered settlers, whose resentment grew into one of the bloodiest range wars in the state's history.

Just as the tensions grew, C.C. Curtis bought a farm along the Okanogan River, a few miles south of the site of present-day Okanogan. He began herding several hundred sheep there and, as forage grew scarce, he moved west toward the Pleasant Valley and Spring Coulee settlements.

Some of Curtis' sheep got into a pasture that a widow used for her milk cows. She asked Curtis to remove his sheep, but he did not.

In the meantime, the cattlemen decided to take their own action against the sheep ranchers. They formed a "Protective Cattle and Horse Raisers' Association," which met twice a month. The association planned to hire some men from outside

The site of the Curtis Sheep Massacre in the Okanogan Valley.

the area to capture the shepherds and kill their sheep. But when the men they found said they would kill the sheep owners if necessary, the association abandoned the idea.

Somehow, Curtis and his sheep became scapegoats for all the association's grievances against the sheep ranchers in Okanogan County. Historical records are not clear on why they picked Curtis, except he probably owned the most sheep in the area. Obviously the person with the largest herd would be considered the cattlemen's biggest threat.

The association sent a delegation to Curtis' farm to reason with him. They convinced Curtis that if he kept his current herd, the spring lambing would increase the flock to about 1,500 and cause great damage to the range. Curtis listened, then promised to sell his sheep and go into general farming.

Curtis kept the promise temporarily. Late in the fall of 1902, he bought another herd of about 1,000 sheep. He wintered them on his ranch, but in the spring, he turned them out on the range east and south of Spring Coulee and Pleasant Valley.

The cattle association met to discuss the problem and decided to kill the sheep on their own. Volunteers would ensure no one revealed the names of those involved in the slaying.

Association members planned to meet on a night in the spring of 1903. Each person would bring a tool that could kill a sheep instantly. A volunteer kept watch on where Curtis was holding his sheep, because the corrals were portable and changed frequently to prevent the sheep from traveling long distances. To cover up the slaughter, the association planned a reception for Dr. Joseph Pogue, a state senator returning from a session in Olympia, the same evening. Most association members, including the man watching the sheep, would attend.

The next day, the association learned that Curtis kept 100 old ewes at home, because they were not strong enough to travel with the herd. Members killed them when darkness fell.

Curtis tried to press charges against the cattlemen, but the prosecuting attorney said he had to produce evidence before the case could be tried—something Curtis could not do. He never raised sheep again and finally left Okanogan County.

Several years after this bloody slaughter, which became known as the Curtis Sheep Massacre, the United States government began regulating the open range. Separate areas were reserved for cattle and sheep herds, and rules were adopted on how to use and manage the range. Ranchers must apply for permits to run livestock on the

The site of the Curtis Sheep Massacre.

range; those who violated the rules would not be allowed to renew their permits. These regulations stopped the struggle between the cattle and sheep owners, and both types of ranching prosper today in the Okanogan Valley.

The Ghost of a Bygone Era

Greenhorn, Oregon

In the early days of mining in northeastern Oregon, an old fellow of slow speech arrived at the tent camp of Robinsonville. Claiming to be a miner, he asked for a job. His experience came from digging potatoes in Missouri and prying wagons from the mud on Pike County highways. He was hired and sent down a shaft to insert a blast into the rock.

After what seemed like hours, he managed to drill a three-cornered hole and pack the dynamite powder into the wall. When he was finished, he yelled, "Haul me up slowly so I can unwind the fuse." He intended to use the entire 50-foot coil he had been given on a 30-foot shaft.

This and a series of similar events gave the man a reputation of a "greenhorn," which became the name of the mining district and mountains surrounding the camp.

The same name was given to a town founded near the Robinsonville site in 1891, almost nine years after the camp was destroyed by fire. But it's uncertain whether the town received the name in honor of the old fellow, because other accounts are just as common.

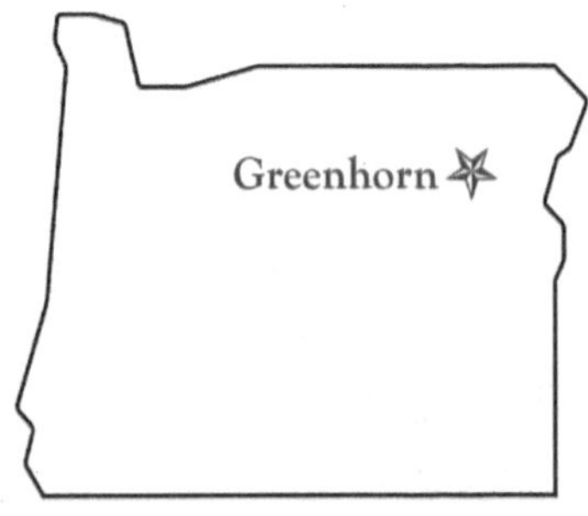

One is that Greenhorn was named in honor of a huge greenish rock perched on a hill overlooking the town. The other is the tale of a trusting young prospector from the east who, as soon as he came into town, asked some old-timers where he should dig for gold. Unenthusiastic about the prospector's interest or company, the man pointed to a tree and suggested, "Why don't you dig there? It's shady and cool."

The young man followed the instructions and struck a rich vein of gold. When he asked whether his find was indeed gold, the men laughed and said, "The poor greenhorn. He doesn't know gold from grass."

Despite the differing stories on how the town got its name, Greenhorn and the surrounding district soon became well-known for their abundance of gold. People flocked there from everywhere to stake claims. During the boom years, 1897-1919, the town of Greenhorn supported 500 residents, and more than 2,000 miners lived in the district. Ten mines revealed rich veins of gold, and three others produced silver-bearing ores.

J.H. Cradlebaugh, a reporter from *The Oregonian*, confirmed the vast quantities of gold when he visited Greenhorn in 1899. "In all my experience," he wrote, "I never saw a country so generally and thoroughly mineralized. Neither have I seen a country where all the adjuncts to successful mining were so plentiful. Water is abundant, timber practically unlimited, and transportation facilities perfect. The country is rough, of course, but the hills present easy grades for roads, and twenty miles from the heart of Greenhorn will take you to Sumpter and the railroad. I make the prophecy now that inside five years the Greenhorn country will be adding to the world's stock of gold at the rate of more than $1 million a month."

No records show if Cradlebaugh's prediction came true, but some very profitable lodes were discovered. By 1902, the Bonanza Mine, the largest in the district, had a shaft 800 feet deep, and work had started on crosscuts at the 700-foot level. One of these crosscuts uncovered a rich vein of gold that soon yielded $20,000 to $30,000 per month. When the mine closed in 1907, the Bonanza had produced a total ore haul of $1,750,000. Other mines were producing gold valued from $7 to $100 a ton.

During the boom years, two hotels, one post office, a water works, several general merchandise and grocery stores, five saloons, a house of prostitution, and a jail lined Greenhorn's only street. The architecture consisted of the high, false fronts typical of the early mining towns. The houses were a mixture of log cabins and frame structures.

At first, all plumbing was outside the buildings at a well and pumping plant. Later, Mayor Simeon C. Richardson devised a new system that gave all homes and businesses cold running water. He asked the state to grant Greenhorn a water right to a spring on a hill one mile west of town. When the state approved, a mile of five-inch wooden pipe was installed, leading from the spring to town. A large wooden container, used as a water storage tank, was built at an elevation high enough to provide adequate water pressure. Those using the system paid a flat charge, which helped keep the system well maintained. The original system operated until the early 1970s, when a new plastic pipe replaced the wooden one.

Mail was delivered by railroad from Tipton, a lumber town near Sumpter. Instead of traveling every day, Postmaster Burton Miller picked up the mail twice a week.

During the first few years of Greenhorn's founding, no law enforcement system existed. Mayor Richardson and E.G. Stevenson kept things under control. They later petitioned the Oregon legislature to have the townsite incorporated. It was approved on February 21, 1903.

The Greenhorn Jail, now located outside the Grant County Historical Museum in Canyon City, Oregon.

After the incorporation, a political problem arose. No one knew in which county Greenhorn was located, because the Baker-Grant county line ran through the middle of the town's only street. Therefore, official incorporation records couldn't show the county location. One Sumpter newspaper reporter wrote, "If some civil engineer with peculiarly keen topographical instincts can go out to Greenhorn and legally establish that the exact division between the drainage of the John Day and Burnt River swings off toward Grant far enough to place the city in Baker, he will receive a premium."

The dispute continued until the town's population declined, when many miners surrendered their land to Baker County for as little as $5 or $10 in unpaid taxes. In 1954, Mayor Richardson, the only resident of Greenhorn from its decline until his death, executed a quitclaim deed to his interests to Baker County. This move awarded the rest of the town to the county. Richardson, however, carried the deed in his pocket until Leona Fleetwood, his niece, talked him into giving it to her. She kept the deed until his death the following year and then turned it over to the Baker County judge.

As more miners moved their families to Greenhorn, the need for a school increased. Although Greenhorn was now incorporated, it was still considered a mining camp, not a legal town. To become legal, the site had to be purchased, surveyed, and recorded. Sites were usually bought through a speculator or from a farmer who wanted to sell land they could no longer use. But no one owned the Greenhorn site, so it had to be bought from the U.S. government.

A group of citizens organized into a "strong mayor" type of government led by Richardson and wrote a letter to Congress requesting purchase. On February 8, 1912, President William Howard Taft issued a patent, granting the site to "Simeon C. Richardson in trust for use and benefit of the occupants of the townsite of Greenhorn and its successors." This government declaration, believed to be the only one of its kind, made Greenhorn a principality, a law unto itself.

But Greenhorn's schooling problem wasn't solved. Oregon state law forbade a schoolhouse to be built within a three-block radius of a saloon. To remain as legal as possible, the town played the game of a "now you see it, now you don't" school, where the children were moved from one building to another. At one time, teacher Kate Mullen held classes in the Red Lion Hotel's lobby. A saloon was in

Above: This historical marker with a brief description of Greenhorn's history was at the townsite when I visited in 2005. When I was there in July 2025, this sign was gone. Below: The only marker I found during my trip in 2025 was this tiny sign at the "city limits."

an adjacent room.

The most popular type of recreation in most mining towns was found at the saloons, and Greenhorn was no exception. Five hundred miners from day shift and 300 from night shift poured into town to be separated from their pokes. Few fights occurred, and no gunfight deaths were recorded.

Every saloon has its own "moocher." In Greenhorn, it was Old Pete, who liked to hang out at the Red Lion Saloon. One night, bartender Jack Marshall offered the lubricated man a pint of whiskey if he would get lost for the rest of the night. Old Pete accepted. Placing the pint in his hip pocket, he walked on unsteady legs through the swinging doors. At the same time, a husky miner burst into the saloon, bumped into Old Pete, and knocked him flat on his back. The bottle of whiskey broke.

After a while, Old Pete felt his wet leg.

"Are you hurt?" the bartender asked.

"By God, I hope so," Old Pete replied.

Other popular forms of recreation included rock-drilling contests, cockfights, dances, horse races, and huckleberry parties. The drilling contests and cockfights drew the biggest crowds.

Rock-drilling contests were held in all mining camps on the Fourth of July and Labor Day. The objective was to determine which team could drill the deepest hole the fastest by using hand drills and heavy jackhammers. The teams, made up of two men each, had 15 minutes to drill holes in a "contest rock." Judges would measure the holes and declare the winners.

In one cockfight, a long-standing champion finally lost. Some spectators discovered the competitor had red pepper on its feet, which managed to get into the loser's eyes.

After the mines failed to produce and the post office closed in 1919, Greenhorn became a ghost town. During the 1960s, several people established summer homes at Greenhorn. Some of them were elected as city officials on January 4, 1971, by a ballot published in the *Democrat-Herald*, a daily newspaper printed in Baker City, Oregon. The city council now has different members, but it still meets periodically.

Today, Greenhorn has an official population of three people, who live there during the summer. The road is closed in the winter because of the heavy snowfall, which makes maintenance impossible.

The last time I visited Greenhorn in July 2025, I noticed two large cabins through the pines that appeared to have been built recently with satellite dishes attached to the roofs and a camper trailer parked nearby that was occupied. The main road through Greenhorn is now named Phoenix Street.

All the old, weathered buildings I saw during my trip in 2005 are gone, except one, and it probably won't last much longer. The only original building in good condition, the Greenhorn Jail, is on display outside the Grant County Historical Museum in Canyon City.

The abandoned mine shafts in and around Greenhorn overflow with memories of a bygone era, and the huge green rock can still be seen nearby.

Above: The Greenhown townsite in 2005. Below: This is the only old building I could find during my trip in July 2025. The elements or humans have wiped out the rest of the buildings.

The Healing Waters of Ea-Kesh-Pa

Hot Lake, Oregon

Long before Caucasians came to eastern Oregon, a tribe of Plains Indians passed through the Grande Ronde Valley on their way to fight the Indians living near present-day Walla Walla, Washington. One of the braves became sick and died at Hot Lake. His companions, eager to fight, tossed his body into the hot, bubbly mud of the lake and left.

When the warriors arrived at Walla Walla, they couldn't find any live enemies. Then, in the distance, they saw a man sitting on a stump. It was the brave they threw into Hot Lake.

The mud healed him, he said. He reached the enemies first and killed them single-handedly.

This legend made the Indians strong believers in the healing powers of Hot Lake. From that time on, the grounds were sacred and used as a hospital and health resort. The Nez Perce called the area "Ea-kesh-pa," meaning "hot place."

Hot Lake was one of the few "absolutely neutral refuges" in the Pacific Northwest, according to Nez Perce Kash Kash. Tribal leaders declared the lake and surrounding valley a place of rest, cure, and peace for the sick and wounded. No battles were allowed. The Indians also drank the water for strength before going to battle.

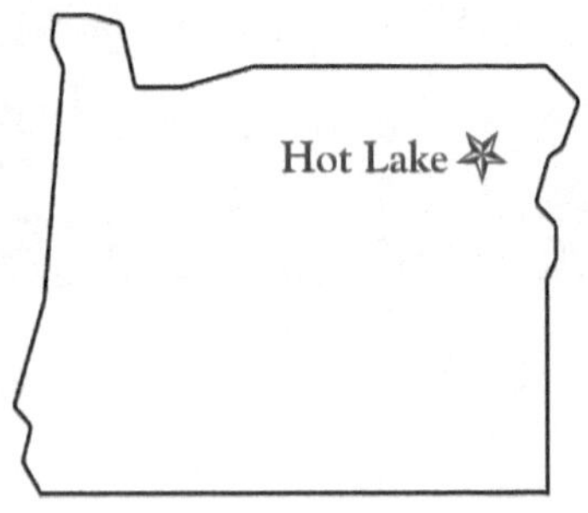

The Indians weren't the only ones to praise the therapeutic values of Hot Lake. After Caucasians discovered the lake, they used the waters to cure all kinds of diseases, ranging from stomach ailments to rheumatism. A resort was built, and by the turn of the twentieth century, thousands of people from around the world flocked there to seek relief from their illnesses.

Hot Lake lies at the southern end of the Grande Ronde Valley near the foothills of the Blue Mountains about nine miles east of La Grande, Oregon. It consists of three lakes separated by a few yards. These lakes are fed by hot springs rising from fault openings that extend 30 miles across the valley. The springs discharge a large quantity of silica, a substance that becomes radioactive after contact with radium.

Two and one-half million gallons of water flow from the springs daily—enough to fill a 90-by-60-foot swimming pool. The water's flow and temperature of 208° Fahrenheit have not varied since the first measurements were recorded in 1878.

Geologists believe Hot Lake may be heated by one of two natural processes that probably occur about 15,000 feet beneath the earth's surface. The water may seep down a fault, where the great depth causes it to boil and rise to the surface. Or it may be heated by a flow of molten rock that started toward the surface but never emerged.

The first white men who saw Hot Lake were 32 members of an expedition led by William Price Hunt. John Jacob Astor, owner of the Pacific Fur Company, sent them west to establish a fur-collection depot at the mouth of the Columbia River, later known as Astoria,

Steam rising from Hot Lake.

Oregon.

When the party entered the Grande Ronde Valley on New Year's Day, 1812, they met a band of Shoshone Indians and exchanged a rifle, musket, and some ammunition for four horses, three dogs, and some roots that they ate for dinner.

On August 7, 1812, Robert Stuart, another employee of the Pacific Fur Company, made the first recorded sighting of Hot Lake. The party he commanded rested there on its way from Astoria to St. Louis, Missouri.

Later, Captain Benjamin Louis Eulalie de Bonneville made notes of Hot Lake in his journals. His comments were rewritten by Washington Irving in a book about the famous explorer's adventures. "In traversing this [Grande Ronde] plain," Irving penned, "they passed close to the skirts of the hills, a great pool of water, three hundred yards in circumference, fed by a sulfur spring about ten feet in diameter, boiling up in one corner. The vapor from this pool was extremely noisome, and tainted the air for a considerable distance. The place was much frequented by elk, which were found in considerable numbers in the adjacent mountains, and their horns, shed in the springtime, around the pond."

Many Oregon Trail immigrants found Hot Lake an inviting oasis after their westward journey through hundreds of miles of hot, dry, sagebrush country. These early pioneers' oxen sought relief from the long walk by soaking their hooves in the hot mud around the lake's edge. Prospectors and freighters also took breaks there because the first trails to the Idaho gold mines followed the same route. The lush, fertile valley was surrounded by pine-covered mountains, streaked with snow from four to six months of the year. Food was always plentiful, even in the winter, and these travelers had a variety to choose from.

Summer fare featured elk, deer, and squirrels, along with an endless assortment of berries and other plants growing on the foothills nearby. Trout abounded in the fresh mountain streams. In the harsher winter months, the wildlife moved closer to the shores of Hot Lake because the snow did not cover the area. Ducks and other water birds made a winter refuge here, and swans stopped and rested during their migrations to Alaska. Wildlife died at the lake in the cold weather when overcrowding created a food shortage.

The first health resort at Hot Lake was built in the 1860s by

Californian Samuel F. Newhard and a Mr. Clark. It included a whitewashed frame hotel, complete with spa and dance hall, and a row of whitewashed frame bathhouses equipped with wooden bathtubs for mud and mineral water treatments. Flowers and poplar trees enhanced the landscape. These buildings stood between the lake and the foothills, facing the foothills. A county road ran along the foothills.

Newhard and his wife gained sole ownership of the resort after Clark's death. During that time, horsemen often bathed in the lakes and used the cattails growing by the shorelines as a dressing room. Newhard never objected to their borderline modesty.

Hot Lake Resort soon gained a reputation as a quality resort, emphasizing rest and relaxation. But an unpredictable stroke of luck contributed to an even faster growth in the number of vacationers visiting the resort.

In 1884, the Oregon Railway and Navigation Company (OR&N) completed a transcontinental railroad line directly passing the resort. This put Hot Lake on the map and helped establish a post office. Newhard served as postmaster for 15 years. Two trains stopped daily.

This piece of the OR&N's route was extremely expensive and did not follow the logical route through Union, the county seat. At that time, the land between La Grande and Hot Lake was swampy, and a route through Union would have provided a better grade out of the valley, bypassing the resort. However, the location was believed to have been selected because of the OR&N's interests in Hot Lake and a battle of egos between the company and Union city officials. Certain records indicate the OR&N held a co-ownership in the resort, but the subject of dispute between the railroad and City of Union is not clear.

Although Hot Lake Resort was prosperous, Newhard apparently lost interest in its continued operation. In 1900, he sold the resort to Dr. H.J. Minthorn, Herbert Hoover's uncle, and Ben S. "Bear" Cook. Both new owners were Quakers. They razed all the existing buildings and replaced them with a new hotel and bathhouses facing the lakes. Hot baths, boating on Hot Lake, and hunting in season attracted the tourists.

Minthorn and Cook met in Newberg, Oregon, in 1884, when Cook and his family moved there from Sheldon, Iowa. Shortly after they met, the formed the Oregon Land Company in Salem. The company's purpose, according to Cook, was to "buy donation land claims, say, at $50 an acre, subdivide them, and sell 10-acre and 20-acre tracts for prune orchards."

When the Oregon Land Company was in operation, Cook moonlighted on several jobs. This work led him and his partner to Hot Lake, as he recalls in a newspaper interview. "I went to work for Bob Hendricks, publisher of the *Oregon Statesman*, the *Pacific Homestead* and various other publications in Salem," he said. "I went up to Eastern Oregon to secure advertising and other business for the *Pacific Homestead* and while there I stopped at Hot Lake. A man named Newhard had taken up this site of Hot Lake as a homestead. He wasn't doing much with it and was rather anxious to let it go. I asked him what he would take for it and he said, 'Somebody can make money out of this proposition; maybe you can. You can have it for $7,500.' I wired Dr. Minthorn at Salem to come down to Portland and meet me at the Perkins hotel. I told him what I thought of the proposition, so he agreed to go in with me, I to take care of the hotel end of it and he to take care of the medical end. We shipped our household goods there at once."

The Hot Lake Springs resort sign waiting to be mounted on the building during my visit there in 2006, when restoration was underway.

The Lodge at Hot Lake Springs in August 2025.

While they owned Hot Lake Resort, Minthorn and Cook turned handsome profits. "The first month we took in $40," Cook said. "We rent it for a year and a half. The last month there we took in $2243.20. We sold out for $20,000." Obviously, the men found the resort profitable enough to choose not to subdivide it for prune orchards!

In the next few years after Minthorn and Cook sold the resort in 1902, its ownership appears to have changed rapidly. Sources disagree on who owned the property and when they owned it; however, owners who were mentioned consistently during this period were a Mr. and Mrs. Tape, remembered for their musical talents and the charming ways in which they entertained their guests. All sources agree that Walter Pierce, a former state governor and U.S. congressman, eventually bought Hot Lake Resort, but the exact year of his purchase is disputed.

In 1906, Pierce spent $500,000 for a three-story brick addition at the eastern edge of the resort's frame structures and called the finished product Hot Lake Sanatorium. It stretched more than 600 feet between the foothills and the lakes, featured a new geothermal heating system, and increased the number of guest rooms to more than 200. Water was pumped in from the lakes to heat the sanatorium.

The top floor of the new wing was used as a hospital and contained a white-tiled, glass-walled operating room, accommodations for 70 patients, and the most modern medical equipment of the day, including X-ray machinery. Guests rented rooms on the second floor. The bottom floor had a cafeteria, medical examination offices, serological and bacteriological laboratories, X-ray and electrical departments, physicians' consultation rooms, a fountain, a ballroom, and a general store. A staff of 175 kept everything going.

Because of its diversity, Hot Lake Sanatorium soon became known as "The Town Under One Roof" and the most popular health resort west of Hot Springs, Arkansas. According to *The Catholic Sentinel*, "So well is this little 'city' organized that it functions with a smoothness which many a housewife in a small bungalow would envy."

Pierce hired Dr. William Phy to manage the hospital. When Phy assumed the position, Hot Lake evolved into a highly respected medical institution, the only one of its kind in the days of the Old West. Many referred to the hospital as the "Mayo Clinic of the West." An average of 4,000 patients were treated each year.

Phy had practiced medicine for three years in Union and several years in Baker City, Oregon, before coming to Hot Lake. A few years later, he bought the sanatorium from Pierce.

Phy was recognized for helping to pioneer many medical beliefs and techniques that are taken for granted today. He advocated the practice of "preventative medicine," which was achieved through an annual physical examination. After these checkups, many patients took several bath treatments to rid their bodies of poisonous substances that might contribute to illness. He was also famous for using the hot water and mud treatments to help overweight people shed pounds and treating cancer with radium and X-rays. Insulin injections to treat diabetes and intravenous hay-fever remedies, routine practices for Phy, were rarely tried by most other doctors of the day.

Phy was one of the first surgeons to successfully use the spinal anesthesia process. Although this method has been virtually abandoned because of its possible side effects, Phy claimed to achieve perfect results after each operation and felt it was more comfortable for his patients.

Phy believed people could maintain their good health by eating a balanced diet of fresh foods and exercising daily. He promoted this idea at Hot Lake by establishing the Phymere Farm. A 30-acre garden produced fresh vegetables, and 50 head of purebred Holstein cattle and 3,000 white Leghorn laying hens provided meat and dairy products. Patients were also encouraged to exercise, when possible, during their stay.

In Phy's view, most doctor visits were unnecessary. "Ninety percent of the people who go to doctors would get well if they were left alone," he told Fred Lockley, a reporter for the *Oregon Journal.* "All they need to do is obey the rules of nature and nature will restore them to health."

Phy and his staff discussed each patient's case, and treatments were either modified or left unchanged. When patients left the sanatorium, Phy gave them instructions on how to continue their own care. These directives always included a diet designed to meet their individual needs. He kept in contact with his patients, even after they returned home.

The treatments varied, depending on the patient's condition, but all included a series of water and/or mud baths.

During a visit to Hot Lake Sanatorium, Lockley decided to take some treatments even though he wasn't ill. "At the entrance to the bathroom," he writes, "I was taken in charge by Al, a Norwegian lad, who for some years followed wrestling as a vocation. He took me through a long room filled with canvas cots, on each of which was a sheet-clad figure. Most of the men on the cots were as red as boiled lobsters and all were sweating profusely. After I disrobed, I was taken to a bathroom and told to step into a tub of water. The moment I stepped in I understood why these men were perspiring so profusely.

"After five or 10 minutes of the hot bath, Al took me to a steam closet, where I stayed for four or five minutes. I think I must have

One of many places to relax inside The Lodge at Hot Lake Springs.

The guest room on the third floor at The Lodge at Hot Lake Springs.

lost a pound or two there for the perspiration was running down my legs in rivulets when I came out. Wrapping a sheet around me, Al pointed to a cot and told me to lie there for 20 minutes or half an hour, and sweat. He didn't have to tell me to sweat, for I couldn't have helped sweating if I had wanted to. From the cot I went to a shower, where the luke warm [*sic*] water was gradually changed to cold. Then I climbed upon a padded table and Al gave me a alcohol rub.

"Next day I reported for a different course of treatment. After taking the tub bath and the steam rub Al rubbed me with eucalyptus oil and cocoa butter and gave me a vigorous massage. The next day I was due for a mud bath and salt rub; but it cost me so much to put on what weight I had I didn't want to lose it all in three or four days, so I took the mud bath and salt rub on faith and watched it administered to others."

Phy frequently treated patients successfully for cardiovascular and renal diseases, such as high blood pressure, heart lesions, and nephritis.

While Hot Lake Sanatorium grew in importance in the medical world, the emphasis on recreation never faded. Current issues of magazines and western metropolitan papers were available at the newsstand at the small store on the first floor. One of the niceties included with each guest's or patient's room was a complimentary newspaper, morning and evening. Patients and guests could play billiards in a room devoted strictly to this purpose.

The most popular gathering places at the sanatorium were the parlors and sun porches, used for reading, card playing, and socializing. Dances were held nightly in the ballroom, and on Sunday evenings a song service was scheduled. Weekly programs featuring talent from patients, staff, and members of the local community were well attended.

In 1932, Phy died after suffering from polio for several weeks. His son, Mark, operated Hot Lake Sanatorium until his death the following year. After Mark's death, the sanatorium quickly lost its reputation as a popular hospital and health resort. Ownership changed rapidly, and on May 7, 1934, a fire destroyed everything except for the brick wing. The buildings were never replaced.

A brief revival of Hot Lake as a destination resort started in 1942, when Dr. A.J. Roth, former professor of bacteriology at Washington State University and member of the Washington State Health Department and Planning Council, bought the property and remodeled the brick wing. Guests rented rooms on the bottom floor for banquets, conventions, and overnight stays. Recreation included hunting, fishing, and hiking. The two top floors were converted into a nursing home.

At that time, a fisherman's story spread about the lake. Roth claimed fish lived there and said in an interview, "It is the only place in the world where you can catch a bass, tow it a few feet, and have it cooked before you take it off the line."

Roth retired in 1974. Ownership of the property changed rapidly again, and the brick building deteriorated. Caretakers watched the property to prevent vandalism, and for decades, no one seemed to be interested in restoring it.

In 1983, a friend who was a caretaker at the property gave me a tour after I wrote a paper about Hot Lake for an assignment in my Pacific Northwest history class at Eastern Oregon State College (now Eastern Oregon University). The damage in the brick building was heartbreaking. All the windows were broken or missing, big chunks of plaster had fallen from the walls and ceiling, and on the third (top) floor, there were large holes in the roof. I wondered whether the building could ever be repaired if anyone tried. But two decades later, someone took on the challenge.

In 2003, David and Lee Manuel from Joseph, Oregon, bought the property and began renovating the building. They worked on it for two years with a lot of help from the community and then opened the building for tours while continuing to renovate the rooms. During a trip to La Grande in 2006, I stopped at Hot Lake and chatted with Lee, and she let me tour the entire building unsupervised. All the windows were replaced and the roof repaired, and some of the renovated hotel rooms were open on the first floor. The decor in each room had different pastel colors and themes, and was beautiful and inviting. Every detail reminded me of stepping back into the early 20th century.

By 2010, the Manuels were operating Hot Lake Springs as a bed and breakfast with the restored rooms and a restaurant, spa, museum, and bronze foundry where David continued creating his famous sculptures. They retired in April 2020 and sold the property to Mike Rysavy, the owner of the Grande Hot Springs RV Resort about a half mile away. He changed the name of the property to The Lodge at Hot Lake Springs and continued the renovations.

Today, all the guest rooms on the first and second floors are available for reservations through Airbnb. All rooms, except two on the second floor, have private bathrooms or half baths with showers. Guests in the other two rooms share a bathroom and shower.

On the third floor, only one room is available. The rest of the floor is still under construction.

On the first floor, lodge guests and the public can watch movies at the theater Thursday through Sunday, and The Thermal Pub serves craft beer, mixed drinks, non-alcoholic beverages, and light fare. Guests can soak in the outdoor thermal tubs next to the lake at no charge, and the public can make reservations for day use for a fee. For more information, go to hotlakelodge.com.

The Lost Wagon Train

Fort Hall, Idaho, to Eugene, Oregon

When the pioneers of the Old West decided to leave their homes in the eastern United States, they made plans far in advance. They consulted settlers who already traveled the long miles and read all available published materials about the journey and the land of their destiny.

But no matter how much they prepared, the unexpected happened. Wagons and harnesses broke. Violent thunderstorms lashed across the plains. Rain soaked through wagon covers, and stops of a day or more were inevitable while the wagons dried. Flash floods caused prairie streams to overflow, filling dry washes within minutes. People were born and died.

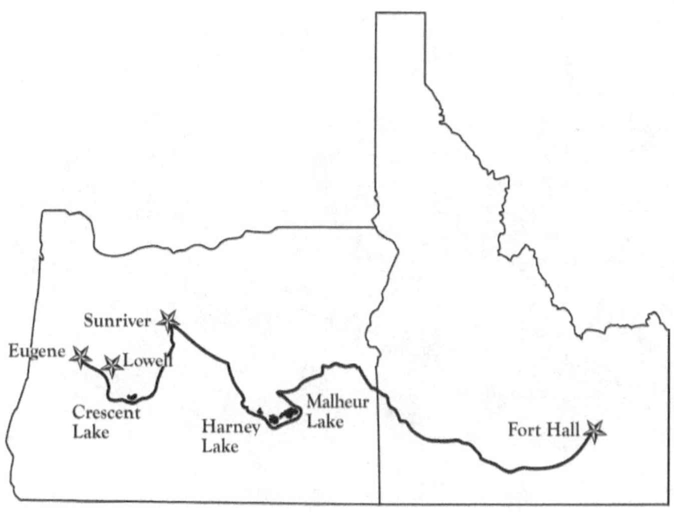

It's no wonder that when a group of immigrants stopped to rest at Fort Hall, Idaho, in 1853, they welcomed Elijah Elliott's news of the Free Emigrant Road, a new, shorter trail across Oregon. Elliott rode from Eugene, Oregon, to Fort Hall in July to meet his wife and children, who were on their way from Fulton County, Illinois, to join him in the southern Willamette Valley. He also was commissioned to bring the first group of immigrants over the new cutoff road, which connected the Oregon Trail directly with the Willamette Valley.

Elliott, a willing and confident guide, did not know the perils he would face on the new trail. He was not familiar with the harsh weather and dry landscape of southeastern Oregon. Neither were the promoters of the road from the Willamette Valley.

"The road is ten to fifteen traveling days shorter than any other route," supporters of the road wrote in a letter published in *The Oregonian* on May 28, 1853. "There is no abrupt or high mountains to cross between Fort Boise and the Cascades, as on the Columbia River route (the Blue Mountains between La Grande and Pendleton); there is an abundance of water and grass, at desirable distances, to supply the largest emigration; there are no large streams to cross; there are no ferries (crossing the Willamette River); no toll gates (at the Barlow Road)....it is an independent, free emigrant road."

It was true that the trail was shorter by about 125 miles, and the terrain was relatively flat between the Oregon-Idaho state line

A replica of Fort Hall in Pocatello, Idaho.

and the Cascades. Water and grass existed, too, but only sparsely in spots miles apart. Between the oases were dry stretches of sagebrush characteristic of the southeastern Oregon high desert.

Compared to the rest of the year, high-desert weather conditions in July and August are at the most extreme. Temperatures can climb as high as 110 degrees during the day and drop into the low thirties at night.

Elliott traveled with the immigrants from Fort Hall to Vale, Oregon, where they arrived on either August 28 or 29, 1853; records are not clear on the exact date. Vale was the turning point, where immigrants decided which road they would take. Twenty wagons followed Elliott onto the new cutoff, while the rest stayed on the old, familiar Oregon Trail.

At first, conditions on the Free Emigrant Road lived up to the descriptions of its promoters. The intersection of the new road and the Oregon Trail was near the Malheur River, a place the Indians favored for its grassy meadows and abundant game.

But after they left the river, the country turned barren. Journeys ranging from 12 to 20 miles a day were sometimes necessary to find even a small source of grass and water. "These long drives without water and grass are very hard on teams," Andrew McClure wrote in his diary. Oxen and horses died from exhaustion. Conditions were equally hard on the immigrants. Provisions shrank, and at least one child and one woman died.

Elliott discovered another problem. Sponsors had assured him that a road to the Willamette Valley would be completed before he could get to the Cascade Mountains, but he found none. The same month that Elliott had left for Idaho, the contractor stopped working on the road because of deep snowdrifts in the Cascades.

A month later, another contractor took over. According to a letter from W.W. Bristow to the *Oregon Statesmen*, the contractor had cut a road from the Willamette Valley to the plains of the Deschutes by October 4, 1853.

Because the road had not been completed on time, Elliott relied on his sponsors' directions. Unfortunately, these directions were confusing and caused the immigrants to spend more time in the desert than necessary. At one point, Elliott told some of the immigrants that he lost the directions, according to J. Marino Gale, a member of the wagon train. But he was confident he could find

Diamond Peak and the Three Sisters, the primary landmarks that would lead them to the Cascades and the refreshing waters of the Deschutes River in central Oregon.

Confusion prevailed, especially after the wagon train reached the Harney Valley and some of the members of the wagon train began complaining about Elliott's leadership. "Under his direction we struck out across the hills and sage plains, heading for the landmarks above mentioned, but bore a little too far south, and experienced much delay and difficulty in passing the lakes [Harney and Malheur] on the south side, whereas we should have kept to the north of them." Gale wrote in a journal after arriving in the Willamette Valley, "Our provisions were well nigh exhausted, and the last stretch before reaching the Deschutes river was not less than seventy-five miles without water. This we made with our weary oxen by traveling all night the last night before arriving there."

The immigrants considered the Deschutes a blessing. Describing the waters as "more delicious than wine," Gale wrote, "...never in my life have I seen a day so intently enjoyed in drinking as was that to us and our poor beasts."

In the meantime, more immigrants had started on the new road, following the lead wagons. By the time Elliott's group reached the Deschutes River on the eastern side of the Cascade Mountains, the population had swelled to 300 wagons.

With little food and the prospect of winter storms, a scout party was chosen to cross the Cascades for help. The first scout reached present-day Lowell on October 16, 1853, and organized a massive rescue effort.

On the other side of the Cascades, the wagon train kept up its struggle toward the mountain pass. "We continued up the River fifty miles before crossing," Esther Lyman wrote in her journal, "and then found the stakes that the road was cut through to the settlements. We were now within 15 miles of the foot of the Cascades where peaks were visible at every opening of the dense forest through which we were traveling....The mountains were thickly covered with pine and cedar. The road was very rough and our teams so weak that we made slow progress....

"Everything seemed to work against us," Lyman continued. "We had only just begun to ascend the mountains when the wagon tongue was broken and had to be toggled up with a pine tree; then

A view of Malheur Lake from the Malheur National Wildlife Refuge headquarters in southeastern Oregon. Elijah Elliott and his wagon train camped here while they were trying to find their way to Eugene in western Oregon's Willamette Valley.

two of our cattle were mired in a ravine and we came very near losing them."

On October 19, the weary travelers met the first members of the rescue party, led by Asahel Spencer, southeast of Crescent Lake. The rescuers brought 20,000 pounds of flour; large quantities of bacon, potatoes, onions, salt, and sugar; and 290 head of work and beef cattle that could draw wagons or be used for food. All the supplies were donated by Willamette Valley residents.

Lyman recalled the meeting in her journal. "I think I was never so glad to see any human being in my life before....you had better believe we had a time of feasting and rejoicing; bread never tasted half so good before although it was made (of) flour, salt, and water. When we had partially satisfied our appetites and turned to thank again our generous benefactor the tears were chasing each other down his cheeks. He hastily dashed them aside and replied that if he relieved our wants he was amply rewarded. Oh, he was a noble young man and the blessings of many a grateful heart will follow him while life lasts."

From Crescent Lake, the rescue party helped 615 men, 412

women and children, 3,970 cattle, 1,700 sheep, 222 horses, and 64 mules make the difficult passage down the Middle Fork of the Willamette River toward Eugene. This last leg of the immigrants' long journey totaled 90 miles, which included crossing the Willamette River and its tributaries 27 times.

When the wagon train arrived in Eugene, the newcomers were housed in abandoned cabins originally used by earlier settlers who had moved into improved living quarters. Eventually, the new immigrants received their own property through the Donation Land Claim Act and settled throughout the Willamette Valley.

The controversy over Elliott's leadership faded after the wagon train arrived at the Deschutes River. By then, the tired immigrants were worried about finding enough food to survive so they could reach civilization on the other side of the Cascades. They didn't have enough energy to dwell on other problems.

Today, Elliott is regarded as a hero because of his willingness to initiate the first journey across an alternate route to western Oregon. Historians claim his efforts helped quadruple the population of the southern Willamette Valley.

For years, the actual path of the wagon train remained a mystery, but in 1983, David Danley, staff naturalist for the Sunriver Nature Center in Sunriver, Oregon, found traces of the trail along the Deschutes River. After searching for traces of the wagon train's trail for several years, Danley spotted the route while inspecting an aerial photograph of Sunriver. The photo showed a narrow avenue of lodgepole pine trees running northeast to southwest from Fort Rock Park across Sunriver to East Cascades Circle Number 11, and toward the meadows along the Deschutes River.

Notes from historic surveyors and an inspection of growth rings in the lodgepole pines confirmed Danley's theory: the passage of the wagons had compacted the area's dry pumice soil, causing it to retain moisture that allowed pine seedlings to take root.

After Danley's discovery, the Sunriver Owners Association designated the trail as a historic site. Danley and a group of Sunriver residents met at the site in 1989 to dedicate a plaque made by C.S. "Red" Palmer to commemorate "Eastern Oregon's Lost Wagon Train," which passed by more than 137 years earlier.

Eugene, Oregon, the lost wagon train's destination. Although Elijah Elliott was criticized for his choice of routes, he is now considered a hero for his willingness to lead the first journey across an alternate route to the Willamette Valley. Back then, immigrants used the Oregon Trail as the westward arterial.

The Pig War

Washington vs. British Columbia

In 1859, Lyman Cutler, originally from Ohio, staked a one-third acre claim on San Juan Island in Haro Strait. The claim was one and one-half miles from Bellevue Farm, owned by British-held Hudson's Bay Company (HBC). One day Cutler paddled his canoe 40 miles to Dungeness, where he spent $10 for a peck of potato seed to start a garden.

His potatoes grew well, and he was proud of his accomplishment. At the same time, a black boar owned by the Bellevue Farm noticed the healthy garden and began a routine of tunneling under the fence, rooting and munching on the baby spuds. Cutler complained unsuccessfully about the pig's persistence to Charles Griffin, the head of the farm.

On the morning of June 15, 1859, Cutler awoke to the sound of a horse trotting past his claim. Looking out the window, he saw a Bellevue Farm employee named Jacob straddling the horse and watching the boar root in the potatoes while the plants were at their best. The angry settler grabbed his gun, ran outside, and shot the pig.

Cutler knew if he did not confess to his act, Jacob would report it. He took the dead boar to Griffin, apologized, and offered $10 compensation; the average price for a live pig at that time was $6.

Griffin refused the offer

and would not accept the apology. "It is no more than I expected," he said, "for you Americans are a nuisance on the island and you have no business here....I shall write to Mr. [James] Douglas [chief factor of HBC's holdings] and have you removed."

"That is not what I came here for," Cutler reminded Griffin. "I came here to settle for shooting your hog."

"The hog is worth one hundred dollars and if you choose to pay that, all right," Griffin said.

That request was more than Cutler could handle. "I think there is a better chance for lightning to strike you than for you to get a hundred dollars for that hog." Cutler also threatened to shoot Griffin if he found him trespassing on his claim, according to a letter Griffin wrote to Douglas later that day.

This argument over a dead pig sparked a much larger conflict. San Juan Island is one of more than 170 islands scattered among the quiet waters between Washington State and Vancouver Island. The Oregon Treaty left the ownerships of these islands unsettled, vaguely locating the international boundary "to the middle of the channel which separates the continent from Vancouver's Island; and thence southerly through the middle of said channel." However, several channels—the Strait of Georgia, Rosario Strait, the Strait of Juan de Fuca, and Haro Strait—lie between the continent and Vancouver Island. In the confusion, each nation interpreted the treaty in its own best interests. The British claimed the international boundary cut through the center of Rosario Strait on the east side of the islands, which gave them control of three of the larger islands, including San Juan, and dozens of the smaller ones. The Americans said the line ran through Haro Strait, west of the islands, which granted them the entire territory.

After Cutler shot the boar, the two governments fought over whether the farmer should be tried and punished, and arguments over which country owned the islands brewed. The British insisted he should appear in court, but the Americans claimed he was only protecting his property.

Shortly after the confrontation between Cutler and Griffin, three British officials—Alexander Grant Dallas, Dr. William Tolmie, and a Mr. Fraser—learned of the incident, and a warrant was issued for Cutler's arrest. (Sources disagree on whether this took place later the same day Cutler shot the pig or the next day.) Dallas, Tolmie, and

The soldiers' tents under the British flag at English Camp on the northern end of San Juan Island, Washington.

Fraser, accompanied by Griffin and Jacob, attempted to apply more pressure on Cutler by unexpectedly stopping at his home.

"Are you the man who shot that hog?" Dallas asked Cutler after he answered the door.

Cutler verified that he was.

"If you do not wish to pay one hundred dollars for the hog, we will take you to Victoria and see," Dallas threatened.

Cutler would not back down. "I do not think you will take me to Victoria if I know myself and I think I do."

"You had better be careful how you talk. The steamer is here and a posse of men. We can take you over with us." Despite Dallas' threats, the British took no action.

When rumors of an impending trial spread, the American settlers tried to persuade Cutler to hide. They knew the tough, opinionated man was a good shot and would not hesitate to kill anyone who might try to arrest him. They wanted to avoid trouble with the British, but at the same time, they wanted to keep their independence. A show of force was not the answer at this point, because any violence could trigger a full-fledged war. Finally, they convinced Cutler to keep out of sight and avoid the authorities.

Word of Cutler's showdown with the boar did not reach U.S. authorities as quickly as it did the British, and then it occurred by accident. On July 9, 1859, General William S. Harney, commander of the U.S. Army in Oregon, ordered the *Massachusetts* to stop in Griffin Bay on its way from Victoria for a routine inspection of San Juan Island's customs station. Paul K. Hubbs, s lawyer, politician, and deputy inspector of customs, met Harney on behalf of the American settlers and complained about the proposed trial of Cutler.

Harney said he could arrange military protection if a special petition were drawn and signed by at least 20 settlers. The petition was written quickly and signed by 22 people, and on July 27, 1859, Harney dispatched Captain George E. Pickett and 60 soldiers from Fort Bellingham, Washington, to San Juan Island. This small company was later reinforced with 350 men. Pickett also issued a proclamation that read, "This [the island] being United States Territory, no laws, other than those of the United States, nor courts, except such as are held by virtue of said laws, will be recognized on this island."

Of course, the British took exception to the proclamation. When they learned American troops were stationed on San Juan Island,

The officers' quarters at American Camp on the southern tip of San Juan Island.

they imported a contingent of the Royal Marines' Light Infantry to ensure their holdings would be recognized. A fleet of five ships carried 2,000 soldiers to the island with orders to prevent more American troops from landing.

Captain Geoffrey Hornby, the leader of the British force, invited Pickett aboard his ship to discuss the situation. The American captain's refusal angered Hornby, and he walked ashore to order the U.S. troops to leave. When Pickett ignored the order, Hornby immediately suggested joint occupation. Pickett also rejected that suggestion, threatening to fight to the last man for this piece of American property.

Hornby returned to his ship and reported the incident to his supervisor, Admiral R.L. Baynes, in Esquimalt, British Columbia. By then, both governments were alarmed at the situation. The United States government sent the army's commander in chief, General Winfield Scott, to San Juan Island to try to establish peaceful relations. During October and November 1859, Scott and Chief Factor Douglas agreed on a joint occupation of the island and cooperative action in repelling any Indian attacks.

The question of who really owned the islands remained unanswered, so a commission was organized to study the Oregon Treaty, but no meetings were held until 1868 because of the American Civil War. In the interim, 100 soldiers from each country were allowed on San Juan Island until the issue could be resolved.

The American troops' base was at Griffin Bay on the south end of the island, and a British camp, now known as English Camp, was established at the north end of the island on Garrison Bay.

The commission could not agree on an international boundary and decided to submit the question for arbitration. They chose Kaiser Wilhelm I, emperor of Germany, as the arbitrator. After three of his top officials thoroughly reviewed all the records, the kaiser established the boundary through Haro Strait, which officially awarded all the islands to the U.S. on October 21, 1872.

Because of the kaiser's decision, Cutler was never tried or convicted for shooting the black boar, nor did he pay any damages. If the decision had turned in the other direction, he might have gone to court.

The memory of this dispute, which became known as the Pig War, thrives on San Juan Island. A bill signed by President Lyndon

This marker at the entrance to English Camp on summarizes the story of the Pig War, a conflict between a farmer and a hungry boar that almost sparked an international incident.

B. Johnson in 1966 established the American and English camps as national historical parks. Hundreds of tourists each year visit those parks and relive the drama that started almost 150 years ago with a disagreement between a man and a pig.

The English Camp Visitor Center is open from May through September, and the American Camp Visitor Center is open from March through November. When the visitor centers are open, you can watch videos about the history of the conflict, view exhibits, and ask questions to the park rangers on duty. The grounds of both camps are open year-round for hiking, short walks, and picnics with scenic views. You might see orca whales, seals, bald eagles, ducks, geese, and other species of birds using the Pacific Flyway.

The Valley of Death

Southeastern Oregon

Peter French is one of the most controversial figures in southeastern Oregon history. Many old-timers claim he had a split personality, but others disagree. French's hired hands respected his aloof, energetic, quick-tempered manner because he was fair to all of his employees. But anyone who got in the way of his expanding cattle empire in Harney County was run down by whatever means possible.

In 1870 at the age of 21, French rode from his birthplace of Red Bluff, California, down the Sacramento River to work in the Willows country for his father's old trail-driving friend, Dr. Hugh Glenn. Glenn liked the youngster's ambitious nature, and two years later, undertook a risk that would become one of his best career decisions. He entrusted French with 1,200 head of white and roan shorthorn cattle, six vaqueros, and a Chinese cook and sent them north to the virtually uninhabited high desert rangeland of southeastern Oregon. French was to claim a piece of land for the newly formed French-Glenn Livestock Company and manage the ranch's affairs, while Glenn provided financial support. Of course, French would receive a percentage of the profits.

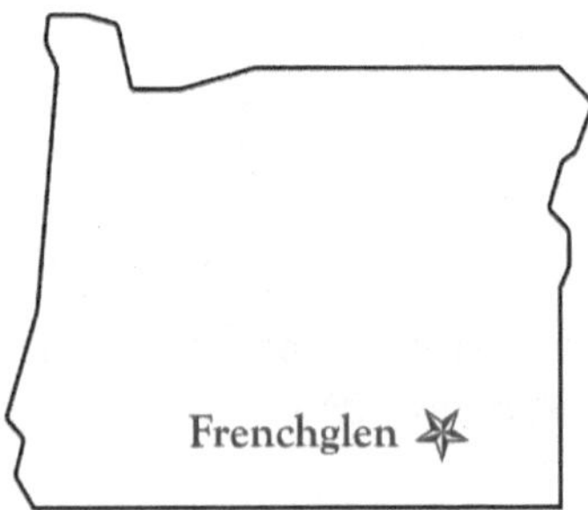

After a two-month journey, French and the vaqueros led the long string of cattle into the fine, bunch-grass country of Catlow Valley in Harney County. They camped at Roaring Springs. There, French bought a brand bearing the letter "P" from a man named Porter,

The Round Barn, designed by Peter French in the late 1800s. The barn was highly regarded for its innovative design.

and the rest stop became a permanent home. The deal included all of Porter's cattle and the land where the herd grazed, which spanned from Roaring Springs to the upper valley of the Donner und Blitzen River.

Every characteristic of this country fired French—the high plateau 4,000 feet above sea level, the giant quantities of native hay, the streams, lakes, and springs, and the sunny, breezy air. He envisioned the valley as a perfect location for raising the highest-quality, disease-free cattle, which, in turn, would produce the largest calves.

On a knoll near the Blitzen River, French built his house, nicknamed the "White House," and willow-thatch corrals. Within a few years, he won control of 200,000 acres of rangeland and thousands of head of cattle.

French could be considered a pioneer in several ranching methods that are used by modern cattle ranchers. He irrigated thousands of acres of sage land with canals and ditches, developed strong fences, and developed unique—but functional—buildings to aid in the daily work around P Ranch.

The fences French and his crew constructed managed to outlive the men who built them. The high desert country has a lot of rimrock, the remains of an ancient geological age when streams cut into the bedrock and left jagged walls of stone to rise above the soil of today's benchlands. Except for occasional breaks, rimrock makes an excellent natural fence, and French was quick to take advantage of that fact. He sent his hands to ride the ridges, looking for breaks, which they plugged with stones or juniper logs.

Juniper posts also made sturdy fences. Wood was a scarce commodity in Harney County, and juniper, deathless in contact with soil, was the usual standby. French and his crew planted these trees several feet apart to use as fence posts. They also cut and dug juniper poles into the ground as far as the rocky soil allowed. Then they bored holes in the poles and strung the wire through.

Because wood was hard to find, French hauled lumber from the Blue Mountains in northeastern Oregon, 150 miles away, to build his "White House" and barns. During construction, 10- and 12-mule teams were constantly on the road pulling wagons filled with boards. The teams continued to arrive long afterward, but now they brought supplies to the ranch from Winnemucca, Nevada, and merchandise for a store French built to accommodate his hands.

French's most admired architectural ideas included his corrals and the round barn. The corrals were built by setting juniper poles at close intervals and binding each with rawhide. Then willow was woven into the framework, similar to weaving a willow basket.

The round barn was used as a shelter where the vaqueros could break horses during the winter months when the snow was too deep in the corrals. Breaking occurred in a 15-foot-wide covered track, which circled the center, or corral, of the barn, 60 feet in diameter. A nine-foot-high stone wall, two feet thick, separated the corral area of the barn from the outer track, which had a 300-foot perimeter. Hewn juniper poles braced the conical, shingled roof, the highest being 40 feet tall and 22 inches in diameter at the base. Another circle of juniper poles 16 feet away surrounded the center pole. An additional 14 feet of space was left between the circle of poles to the sturdy rock wall. The rock wall consisted of a series of square openings at regular intervals about breast height above the dirt floor.

Some authors who have written about French speculate these openings were strategically placed because he thought about using the barn as a stronghold against the Bannock and Paiute Indians,

The juniper support beams for the roof of the Round Barn.

who often fought the settlers, but this isn't the case. These openings helped ventilate the interior of the barn.

French and his crew had one confrontation with the Paiutes. They were in the middle of the spring roundup at Diamond Ranch when Coon Smith, another settler, rode in fast from Happy Valley.

"The Indians are coming!" he shouted.

Close behind Smith, French could see the scouting party tearing down Diamond Hill. He yelled for his crew, who were working in a corral, to grab their horses and head for P Ranch. While the men made good their escape, he jumped to the top of the corral, grabbed Smith's rifle and single box of cartridges, and shot at the advancing Indians.

Another view of the juniper support beams inside the Round Barn.

French knew the Indians would attack again, probably where McCoy Creek Trail ran through a gap in the ridge. He leapt on his horse and sped to the gap, arriving just in time to hide behind a rock and shoot at the oncoming Paiutes.

The young cattleman's quick thinking helped his vaqueros and Smith reach P Ranch safely, but the Chinese cook accompanying the crew was not as lucky. When the Indians attacked, the terrified cook fell from his horse, and a brave shot and scalped him seconds later.

After a short break, French and his crew decided to flee to the sanctuary of Camp Harney, almost 100 miles from the home base of P Ranch. When they arrived, General O.O. Howard appointed French as a courier and set out with a group of soldiers and civilian volunteers to track the Paiutes. They found the OO Ranch burned and many of its horses stolen, but the P Ranch had managed to stay intact.

The cavalry found the warriors at Silver Creek and fought an indecisive pitched battle. As French watched the struggle from behind General Howard's lines, he caught sight of a brave riding one of his favorite horses. Angry, he galloped up and down the line offering a reward to anyone who would shoot the horse's rider. No one accepted.

Late March or early April began the busiest season of the year for French and his vaqueros. First, the cattle that had wintered in the valley were driven to the range. Next came the roundup of the horses and branding of the colts. When that was done, they rounded up the cattle and branded the unweaned calves.

Crews from all the surrounding ranches, whose cattle shared the range, worked together, separating the cows and their calves. The hands worked hard, but sometimes they had time for impromptu bucking and roping contests. The camp cooks fed them well.

French was not only a good architect and hard worker, but he was also an excellent businessman who was not afraid to take risks. He originated a marketing method that would be practiced in southeastern Oregon for a long time. In late November or December, he bought steers from other cattlemen and homesteaders, strictly on credit. He drove them with his own herd to Winnemucca to ship by rail to San Francisco. There he sold the stock, and in January, he returned with a satchel full of gold.

All of French's inventions and business strategies paid off. In the

The circular walkway inside the Round Barn. The vaqueros used it to train and exercise horses.

1880s and 1890s, Harney County gained a reputation in the large markets for producing high-quality, disease-free livestock. Before the railroad, the cattle were trailed east, and most of the ranches of Wyoming and Montana were stocked from those herds. Harney County herds outsold Texas cattle practically everywhere.

Despite all of his hard work, French did manage to maintain a social life. The White House was always open to guests, who were many. Cattlemen from three states often dropped in on French. Their brands were burned into the wood around the fireplace as decoration. A big table was invariably set, and two cooks were always ready to provide meals for any number of people.

French also managed to indulge briefly in romance. In February 1883, he traveled to San Francisco and married Dr. Glenn's daughter, Ella. But the marriage seemed destined to fail. The first indication came 16 days after the wedding when Dr. Glenn died, murdered by ex-bookkeeper Huram Miller. Miller accused Glenn of cheating his California field hands of their wages.

The emotional and economic strain of losing her father, along with her inability to adapt to the isolated, rugged atmosphere of Harney County, caused Ella to file for divorce in 1891. She enjoyed her role in San Francisco's high society, and many believe she never spent any time in Harney County during the marriage; however, the marriage produced a son who lived with Ella and adapted to her familiar lifestyle.

Despite French's distance from his son, he still loved children, and several youths of his day had fond memories of the famous cattleman. In a newspaper interview, "Bruss" Byrd recalled one favorite moment. "He took me to his ranch when I was a little shaver," he said, "talking along and visiting in a chummy way. I remember an old chair in the 'White House' made of cows' horns. The legs and feet were of hoofs, the arms were horns. But wasn't I proud when he told me I could sit in it!"

Grover Jameson, another pioneer, said, "Every time he'd come to town [Burns], he'd drive into the livery stable here on Main Street and count how many there were of us and say, 'Now you boys stay right here. I'll be back in just five minutes....'

"He'd go across to the saloon, and if there were twenty kids there, he'd get twenty silver dollars and come over and give each kid a silver dollar apiece. Well, naturally, when Pete French came to town it was the Fourth of July with we [*sic*] kids."

Cattle are still a common sight in southeastern Oregon, because ranching remains a major industry there. I spotted these cattle near the eastern border of the Malheur National Wildlife Refuge.

The losses of Dr. Glenn, Ella, and his son triggered a series of problems for French that originated in California and spread to the P Ranch. The worst was the financial strain of his family's lifestyle. When Glenn's died, his estate was valued at $1,232,000, but all of it was encumbered by debt. The P Ranch was the only successful venture of Glenn's career; it supported his failures in California and his lawyers.

At the same time, nature was reacting unfavorably to French's irrigation ditches. Malheur Lake, where the Donner und Blitzen River drained at the far northern end of the P Ranch, began refilling. The waters lapped at a sand reef that had blown in across the overflow channel into landlocked Harney Lake and the alkaline flats on the west.

During the late spring of 1881, the reef washed out—helped by a little human intervention, according to some stories—and the water level of Malheur Lake dropped nearly a foot. About 10,000 acres of lake-bottom lands were exposed, mostly adjacent to the 1877 meander line that marked the boundaries of P Ranch.

Settlers began moving into Harney Basin, looking for land they could farm. They naturally drifted to the floodplain, which was level, open, and inviting to the plow.

Not only did the new fertile land around Malheur Lake attract newcomers, but it also opened a hornet's nest. Under English common law, the owner of a shoreland is given ownership to the middle or center thread of a stream or lake, in accordance with the doctrine of riparian rights. But at the time the floodplain was first exposed, French did not know about those rights. The settlers filtered in until August 1894, when French returned from consulting his lawyers and the heirs of the Glenn estates.

Determined to keep the property that legally belonged to the P Ranch, French immediately sent letters requesting the settlers to vacate. The settlers paid little attention to the letters, and French began a lawsuit in the federal court in Portland. The federal court transferred the lawsuits to the Harney County circuit court in Burns, and time passed while relations between French and the settlers steadily deteriorated.

Because of the vast number of lawsuits, French asked the settlers to choose one case that would decide the entire issue and lessen their court costs. They rejected the idea, but the court used the *French-*

Glenn vs. Springer dispute as the test case.

During the trial, French testified that Alva Springer had built on a knoll, cut hay, and deprived him of using land worth 50 cents an acre to the French-Glenn Livestock Company. He also claimed he had demanded possession of the land numerous times. Springer said French had encouraged him to settle there, but despite the welcome, French's crew had shot at him. Springer was not hurt, but his horse caught a .45 bullet in its front hoof.

Despite the conflicting testimony, the jury decided in favor of the settlers, probably because there were more of them. Businessmen in Burns needed the community's trade, and the majority of settlers on homesteads or claims throughout Harney County's 10,132 square miles resented the richer cattle barons.

Unsatisfied with the verdict, desperate, and angry, French appealed. Public hatreds ran even deeper, which caused acts of revenge and violence. Horse herds were run off, leaving women and children afoot. Miles of P Ranch fence were cut, and haystacks were burned.

Rumors of gangs and conspiracy developed. One was that a group of homesteaders met and agreed French must be killed. They secretly drew straws for the duty—and honor. While nobody knew whether this story was true, everybody wondered who was packing the short straw.

Another rumor involved Rye Smith, a settler in Diamond Valley, well liked and trusted by the community. One evening at the end of a party, while Smith and his wife were gathering their sleeping children from a bedroom, George Miller tried to stab him. Smith shot a bullet through Miller's mouth and out the side of his cheek. The two men became friends afterward, and Miller confessed that French had hired him to kill Smith.

Through all the struggles, French's crew supported and continued to respect him. They admired the cattleman's talent for treating every hand fairly. Although French expected them to earn their pay, he worked as hard as any of them. Often, he rehired men who had quit after a foreman made unreasonable demands, and he kept the crew on after the winter drive, although there wasn't much work to do.

Unfortunately, the support from French's crew would not save him from his final fate. Ed Oliver, who had a history of violence and grievances, lived on property one mile south of Rockford Lane, a public road running east and west through French's property. Oliver's homestead was inside French's boundary fence, and French demanded $500 for a right of way to Rockford Lane. Oliver could not afford to pay, but he probably would not have paid if he could.

French threatened Oliver publicly, saying something to the effect of, "I'll fix you good if I ever catch you on my property." Oliver ignored French's warning and took some cows to the homestead south of Rockford Lane.

On Christmas Day, 1897, French returned from a business trip in Chicago with a buckboard full of gifts for his crew's children. He distributed the gifts that night at a Christmas party at the Sod House Ranch. Chino Berdugo, the boss of the drive that was to start the next day, became ill sometime during the party. French told him to take the buckboard and team back to the P Ranch, where he could rest until he felt better.

The next morning, French took Berdugo's horse and assumed the role of crew boss. Finding the horse a little slow, he stopped and cut a willow rod to aid his spurs. Later, to help urge the cattle on in the cold winter weather, he made a whip by attaching a string of buckskin to the willow rod.

As they approached the gate to the big sagebrush field, French rode around the cattle to open the gate. After throwing back the

Malheur National Wildlife Refuge in southeastern Oregon, where Peter French and his vaqueros ran cattle in the late 1800s. This panorama is from the Buena Vista Viewpoint.

gate and remounting his horse, French entered the field so the cattle would follow.

Suddenly, he saw Oliver on his horse, galloping out of a swale. Oliver headed straight for French and charged. The horses crashed with such force that French's mount fell to its knees. French struck Oliver's horse over the head in an effort to fend off his assailant. Oliver charged again, and French responded by striking him over the head and shoulders with the willow whip, according to Emanuel Clark, one of French's riders who was the closest to the scene.

Oliver pulled the gun from his waistband and waved it. French rode a few yards away, then looked back. As he turned, Oliver fired, hitting French in the right cheek. The bullet passed through his head, emerging behind the left ear, and killed him instantly. Oliver rode past French's body and headed west at a fast clip.

Dave Crow, another of French's hired hands, also witnessed the shooting. Within minutes, he left for Winnemucca to spread the news. He rode first to the P Ranch to change horses, then headed out over the trail south that led through Fields, at the lower end of the Steens. Crow reached Winnemucca in 43 hours, stopping only to change horses.

Meanwhile, a coroner's jury had convened at the Sod House Ranch and concluded French died from gunshot wounds inflicted by Oliver.

Newspapers gave generous space to the death of the well-known cattleman, but some of the stories were distorted. The Burns paper, which seldom spoke favorably of French, covered the murder in a few words on an inside page. It also defended the county against a charge by *The Oregonian* that Oliver's $10,000 bail was too low, adding that local sentiment seemed to favor the killer.

And favor it did. Despite the overwhelming evidence of Oliver's guilt, the jury found him innocent.

The settlers soon learned that French had not been the cause of their problems. Oliver merely killed their scapegoat, and now they had to assume responsibility for their own woes. The variety of crops they could grow was still limited; the railroad was just as far away; and the transportation was slow. Competition with the large stockmen had not ended, nor had competition among themselves. Regardless, the settlers held onto their land. They continued quarreling and, ironically, developed the same attitude about riparian rights that caused French's death. Some who held land abutting the meander line tried to invoke the law of riparian rights and exclude others who settled beyond it.

Oliver grew increasingly arrogant by attempting to bask in the role of hero, but the reaction of the more thoughtful members of the community prevailed as his popularity faded. Eventually F.C. Lusk, executor of the French estate and manager of the French-Glenn Livestock Company, purchased Oliver's land. On October 11, 1898, Oliver's wife filed for and received a divorce. She remarried a year later and lived a long, respected life in eastern Oregon. Oliver finally left the country.

Eventually, the French-Glenn Livestock Company was sold to Swift & Company, which decided the land was unprofitable and sold it for $675,000 to the federal government in 1935 for an addition to the Malheur National Wildlife Refuge, which was established by President Theodore Roosevelt in 1903.

A million birds a year—including ducks, geese, grebes, killdeer, avocets, and many other species—nest peacefully in the marshes where Peter French dug canals, built dams, and argued with homesteaders. A small number of trumpeter swans, once almost extinct, are guarded zealously by refuge staff.

Today, thousands of bird lovers visit the site of the old P Ranch to observe, study, and take pictures. Countless others are drawn to the valley by the romance of the early days when one man, through ambition and ability, carved a cattle kingdom. Several landmarks from those lively times remain, including French's Round Barn, the Sod House Ranch, and the Frenchglen Hotel & Drover's Inn.

Local ranchers Richard and Thomas Jenkins deeded the Round Barn with two acres of land and an access easement to the Oregon Historical Society in 1969. The historical society gave the property to the Oregon Parks and Recreation Department in 1995. The barn is open for self-guided tours year-round. The Jenkins family operates a visitor's center near the site's entrance with a museum and gift shop.

The Sod House Ranch, now owned and managed by the U.S. Fish and Wildlife Service as part of the Malheur National Wildlife Refuge, is open from August 15 through October 1. Eight of the original buildings are still standing: the homestead house; a two-story bunkhouse; the Long Barn, designed by French and built in 1888; a two-room office, a stone cellar, a hide shed, a harness shed, and a chicken coop/carriage shed/grain storage building.

Today, Frenchglen Hotel & Drover's Inn is a state historic site. It's owned by the Oregon State Parks and Recreation Department and managed by concessionaires. It has eight guest rooms and a dining room, and reservations are accepted from mid-March through late October.

The Frenchglen Hotel & Drover's Inn is open to guests from mid-March through late October. The Oregon State Parks and Recreation Department owns the hotel, and concessionaires manage it.

The Wildest Town in Oregon

Copperfield, Oregon

Fern Hobbs' brief visit to Copperfield, Oregon, left a lasting impression. It closed the town.

Copperfield was near the Oregon-Idaho border on the west bank of the Snake River at the end of a tortuous, 60-mile railroad branch from the main line at Huntington. At first it was a quiet community, a tent camp originally named Copper Camp by the prospectors who arrived there in 1900. But when two nearby construction projects started in 1909, Copperfield blossomed like a poisonous flower in the northeastern Oregon desert. The town existed mainly to satisfy the uninhibited appetites of more than 2,000 men working on a railroad tunnel and a power plant.

Four businessmen from Baker City drew up plans in 1908 to build Copperfield on a rocky, 160-acre hillside. They invested $10,000 in the venture and within six months received more than a 400 percent return. Later, they sold their remaining holdings for $7,500.

In less than a month after the construction projects began, Copperfield gained a reputation as the most rowdy town in Oregon. Outsiders affectionately referred to it as the "Gomorrah on the Snake."

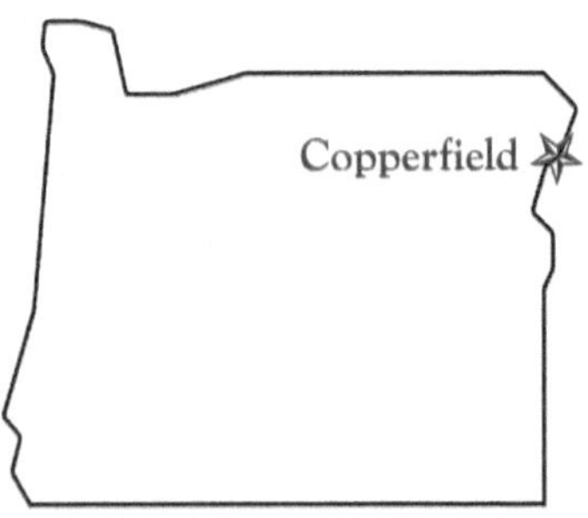

Eleven saloons, 11 disorderly houses, and several gambling dens provided unlimited entertainment. Drunken men, lying like railroad ties in the winter snows and blistering summer sun, were a common sight. On Independence Avenue, the main street, it wasn't unusual to see a dozen fights at once between the two construction crews. They fought with rocks and bottles, and although there were many injuries, no deaths occurred.

Independence Avenue was named appropriately, because Copperfield had no law system, and most residents were proud of this. The nearest sheriff and jail were in Baker City, 150 miles away by railroad. No arrests were ever made.

Copperfield's remoteness allowed for all kinds of vice and debauchery, along with attracting a variety of parasites. According to a Portland newspaper, "if things became too hot in either state it was easy to cross the Snake into the other, and it [Copperfield] was so generally 'onery' that Baker county [*sic*] officials...considered it unworthy their troubling themselves about."

Rowdiness and lawlessness reigned in Copperfield until 1913, when the construction projects were completed. Because fewer men were working, competition for the remaining trade became stiff. Saloonkeepers began feuding.

Suddenly, one night in May, the saloon owned by Martin Knezevich and an adjoining hotel burned to the ground. He and his wife barely escaped. Knezevich rebuilt his saloon nearer the new power plant to attract business from the farmers who drove from Pine Creek to Copperfield. At the time, he had no idea how much controversy his new business would create.

Without warning, the faction to which resident William Weigand belonged decided to incorporate Copperfield as a city. A dubious election produced H.S. Stewart, a saloonkeeper, as mayor. Tony Warner, Stewart's partner; Charles Kuntz, Weigand's bartender and handyman; and Weigand took the councilmen seats. Their first official act was to issue liquor licenses to every saloon except Knezevich's, whose establishment was declared outside the zone where the city allowed saloons to operate.

Knezevich was fined $35, which he refused to pay. The city marshal tried to arrest him, beat him over the head with a revolver, and then gave up. Knezevich took his case into court, but lost.

Knezevich then complained to the Baker County prosecutor, who traveled to Copperfield, stayed between trains, and returned to Baker. He said because the town was so full of wrangling and threats, he could not get to the bottom of the problems.

A view of the Snake River from the village of Oxbow, Oregon. This stretch of the river forms the Oregon-Idaho border. When Copperfield was booming nearby, it was easy for lawbreakers to cross the border here and wait for the heat to subside before slipping back into town unnoticed.

Unsatisfied, Knezevich appealed to Ed Rand, Baker County sheriff. Rand also went to Copperfield, looked around, and returned to his office. He claimed he could make neither heads nor tails of what was happening there.

Knezevich's new saloon caught fire the following November and was saved from total destruction by the quick work of him and his friends. At the same time, a fire was found burning in the back of Weigand's saloon. Both had been carefully prepared with oil-soaked kindling.

The city officials blamed Knezevich for setting the fires and using his own as a "blind." Knezevich denied the charges, claiming the Stewart-Weigand faction was responsible.

In the meantime, several complaints and a petition signed by 55 residents in and near Copperfield were sent to Oregon Governor Oswald West. Mothers mourned their sons, who were being dragged into the "hellholes of the Snake." Others demanded respectable city leaders who would be more interested in upholding morals and justice than peddling liquor and encouraging prostitution.

Another common concern centered on the saloonkeepers selling alcohol to boys ages 14 to 18. Several boys claimed they bought drinks at Warner's and Weigand's saloons whenever they chose, even on Sundays. Harold Burns testified at an injunction hearing that he took $2.50 from his mother, used it in gambling and slot machines, and then became drunk in the mayor's saloon.

Other boys said they could get liquor by stopping at a furnishings store, which operated in the back of Weigand's saloon, and asking for a pair of "shoes." The shoes, a bottle of beer or a flask of whiskey, would be waiting for them on one of the shelves.

These reports and complaints outraged Governor West. He wired Sheriff Rand and ordered closure of Copperfield by Christmas Day 1913. Nothing happened. Copperfield celebrated Christmas in the usual style—drinking, gambling, fighting, and whoring.

Oxbow, Oregon. The rowdy mining-construction town known as Copperfield was founded near this village in 1908. Six years later, Governor Oswald West sent Fern Hobbs, his personal secretary, and a contingent of National Guardsmen to close the saloons after the Baker County sheriff failed to restore law and order here. Today, most of the residents work for the Idaho Power Company, which owns the Oxbow Dam across the main road from the village.

West had a reputation, too. He was a governor of determination and a man of his word. When he set a goal, he made sure it was achieved, and often the outcome was dramatic.

Verbal sharpshooting started crisscrossing the state, primarily through the media. The major wire services started following the story, and soon most of the world knew about the controversy.

Mayor Stewart said things were not out of hand in Copperfield, and those who signed the petition did not know what they had signed. When news reporters asked those people about this, they denied Stewart's accusations and said they were glad they signed the petition.

Sheriff Rand told West he couldn't do anything to control Copperfield because it was a city with its own government. West replied that the town had no government; it was being run by and for a bunch of underworld characters.

Because Rand would not cooperate, West decided to step in and clean up Copperfield in his own way. In an interview with the *Oregon Journal*, he said, "[the Baker County officials assure] me they have nothing but the best intentions and not for the world would they knowingly tolerate violations of the law. They say they realize Copperfield should be closed up but they can't see where they have the authority to do it.

"I want to say that we are told that hell is paved with good intentions....If the sheriff and district attorney can't close the Copperfield saloons, I guess I will have to send Miss Hobbs."

Fern Hobbs, West's private secretary, was a self-reliant person and had made her own way since high school. After she moved from her parents' ranch in Nebraska to Oregon in 1904, she worked as a governess for a Portland banker's family and studied stenography. She later studied law while working as secretary to the president of a title guarantee company. In 1913, she was admitted to the Oregon State Bar. West hired her as chief stenographer and soon promoted her to private secretary.

Shortly before West announced he would send Miss Hobbs to Copperfield, she returned from what the *Oregon Journal* called "an important mission to Washington, DC." No details of her trip were available, except "she surprised many with her ability in handling state matters pending before Congress and various governmental departments."

West pointed out that although Sheriff Rand was six feet six and weighed more than 200 pounds, he admitted that he wasn't big enough to handle Copperfield. "My secretary Miss Hobbs," West said, "is five feet three and weighs 104 pounds."

After Mayor Stewart heard West's announcement, he told the Associated Press, "We are decorating the city with ribbons and will try to have some flowers for Miss Hobbs."

West replied that flowers were appropriate. After all, weren't they traditional at funerals?

On January 1, 1914, West asked Miss Hobbs to prepare resignations for the mayor and councilmen's signatures. He also dictated a proclamation of martial law and told Miss Hobbs to take the documents to Copperfield, along with six national guardsmen. Then she would call a meeting.

"At the meeting," he said, "you will call upon city officials who are in the saloon business for their resignations. If they refuse, you are to declare martial law, disarm everybody in town, close the saloons, and ship all liquor, bar fixtures, and gambling equipment out of Copperfield."

West's strategy to close Copperfield hadn't been released to the press, but, during an interview of Miss Hobbs the night she left for Copperfield, a reporter from *The Oregonian* made a valiant but unsuccessful attempt to find out what would happen.

"Are you armed?" he asked.

"Armed?" she replied. "Well, yes; I am. I have a dressing bag, a portfolio, and an umbrella. I don't believe I could do much with these. Do I look like a Carrie [*sic*] Nation to you?"

(Carry Nation, also known as "Hatchet Granny," was a radical member of the temperance movement known for smashing saloons with a hatchet before Prohibition.)

"How do you propose to proceed?" the reporter asked.

"Well," she said, smiling. "I guess I will proceed to Baker and from there to Copperfield."

"When you get to Copperfield, what are going to do?"

"Close the saloons."

"How are you going to do it?"

"I don't think it is well to tell how you are going to do things before you do them."

"How long will you be in Copperfield?"

Oxbow Dam, a hydroelectric concerte dam on the Snake River with a 700-foot spillway and three gates. The dam, owned by the Idaho Power Company, was built in 1961 and is rated at 220,000 kilowatts. The name originates from the early settlers in this area, who said this part of the Snake River reminded them of the U-shaped collars worn by oxen.

"I will be there between trains, perhaps a couple of hours."

"And you expect to close the saloons in that time?"

"I do for a fact. Maybe it won't take that long."

When Miss Hobbs and the six guardsmen arrived at Copperfield the next day, the entire population was waiting at the depot. The townspeople followed them to the dance hall, where Miss Hobbs asked for the saloonkeeper-officials' resignations. All refused to step down. Then, Colonel B.K. Lawson of the National Guard proclaimed martial law and arrested Mayor Stewart and his councilmen. He also confiscated everyone's weapons after the meeting. More than 170 revolvers were taken.

The drama was not limited to the dance hall. While Miss Hobbs and Colonel Lawson carried out Governor West's orders inside, the other guardsmen were outside, boarding up every saloon and gambling house. By the time the meeting ended, each building had a bold, official "Do Not Enter" sign tacked to its closed door.

More than 100 cases of beer; two roulette tables, several faro tables and slot machines, and a variety of chips and other gambling paraphernalia were loaded in boxcars and shipped to Baker City. Some of the slot machines had been used so recently that the change had not been emptied from the coin holders. Amounts ranging from $5 to $20 were found in each machine.

What would happen to Copperfield's spoils was not clear. Newspaper reporters speculated everything would be shipped to Portland, where the liquor would be sold or destroyed and the gambling machines burned.

The next day, West sent 10 extra guardsmen to Copperfield in case any more trouble broke out. At the same time, the ousted city officials began wiring threats of lawsuits and injunctions. Colonel Lawson ignored them and stationed a guard over the telegraph to prevent messages from being sent or received. Laster, he held a meeting in the dance hall to form a provisional government and appointed Sam Grim, a carpenter, as mayor.

The quick closing of the saloons, gambling dens, and prostitution houses in Copperfield created a completely different atmosphere. A few days after Fern Hobbs returned to Salem, the state capital,

The Oxbow Visitor Information Center, a wayside on the Oregon side of the Snake River. The Copperfield marker at the right of this shelter is the only evidence the town ever existed.

the *Oregon Journal* reported, "There's nothing to do here now but stand around and look at the soldiers, as even hunting, the favorite recreation of the people of Copperfield when all other amusements fall, is barred by the fact that every gun in Copperfield is under guard in the city jail. And the sports of the place are lamenting that fact that not for years have so many rabbits, bobcats, coyotes, and birds been seen hereabouts as in the past week.

"At least two of the former saloon keepers, William Weigand and Martin Knezevich, have been converted by the governor and are going to quit the business altogether, they say, while the other two, ex-Mayor Stewart and his partner, Tony Warner, are still so dizzy from the effects of the whirlwind closing up of Copperfield that they have not dared make plans for the future."

Copperfield did not survive long enough to determine if higher moral standards would prevail. Its population shrank to 50, and in August 1915, a fire destroyed the town. The only remaining building was a schoolhouse on the hill. When Copperfield was annexed to the Homestead District in 1945, the school was sold to a group for $1. It was resold two years later to a man who tore it down for materials.

Today, the only evidence of Copperfield's existence is a marker at the Oxbow Visitor Information Center, a wayside that overlooks the Snake River. The village of Oxbow thrives quietly near the original site of Copperfield. Most of the residents are employees of the Oxbow Dam, which straddles the Snake River across the main road from the village. The dam, built in 1961 as part of the Hells Canyon Project, helped transform the river into a major hydroelectric producer.

Wallace's Silver Years

Wallace, Idaho

In 1884, Colonel W.R. Wallace, a Civil War veteran, built a cabin on an 80-acre tract near the south fork of the Coeur d'Alene River in Idaho Territory to serve as his mining exploration headquarters. His hired hands used the land around the site as their base camp, and the community became known as Placer Center. But that changed when the colonel's wife arrived.

Lucy Wallace came to northern Idaho in 1885, accompanied by a dog, a bird, some cats, and chickens. She became postmistress in August 1886. After her appointment, she announced that the U.S. Post Office Department would not accept the name of Placer Center because it was too long. She wanted to name the town after her husband, but he objected because he believed there were too many towns already called Wallace. Despite his opinion, Lucy completed the postal department slip, listing the post office in the colonel's name.

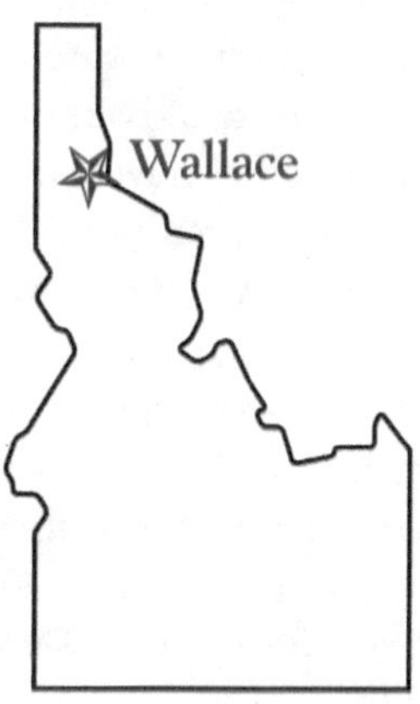

Within a year after Lucy submitted the application, Wallace's population grew to 500. News about gold and silver discoveries attracted drifting prospectors and unemployed men who settled there and wrote letters to their wives, asking them to come along and bring the children. That same year the town's first newspaper, the *Wallace Free Press*, printed its premier issue. It stated that the early history of Wallace was much too well known to be described in print.

Wallace's location at the confluence of five major canyons made it a natural trading center for the rapidly expanding Coeur d'Alene Mining District. The town was also near the towns of Wardner, Davenport (later known as Gem), Murray, Burke, and Mullan. In 1887, enough business existed in Wallace for a general store, sawmill, saloon, livery stable, boot and shoemaker, paint shop, dairy, and two butcher shops to operate. Even contractors, notaries public, a doctor, assayer, mineral surveyor, and justice of the peace were available. But the town's blessing was also a hindrance. The deep canyons, flanked by mountains covered in dense forests, were a paradise for bandits and robbers.

The first recorded robbery occurred on August 5, 1887. E.J. Catlett, a freighter, left Burke the previous afternoon and camped near Glidden Summit. The next morning he awoke with intentions of going to Thompson Falls, but three highwaymen stopped him. Two held him at gunpoint while the third took his cash, a total of $135. The robbers escaped on the divide between Prospect and Canyon Creeks and were never found.

Less than two weeks later, one highwayman robbed three men on the Murray-Thompson Falls Road. The victims lost $540, two watches, a ring, and $2,000 in a package belonging to the Bank of Murray. Although the Bank of Murray announced rewards of $100 for the robber and $500 for the return of the money, neither was ever found.

These problems were solved as growing silver, lead, and zinc discoveries attracted railroad developers to the Coeur d'Alene Mining District. Ore could be shipped from the mines easier, local merchants could obtain goods from eastern wholesale houses quicker, and personal travel would be much safer and faster.

On September 30, 1887, a large crowd greeted the first train on the new narrow-gauge railroad, which ran from the Mission of the Sacred Heart at Cataldo to Wallace. Rain that day did not dampen the celebration, which was originally scheduled outside. Speechmakers moved to the first floor of the Carter Hotel and a grand ball followed their presentations.

More track was laid as more mines opened. The *Wallace Free Press* reported that Davenport Mayor J.H. Jackson ran a first-class saloon in Davenport, and all trains would stop there for 15 minutes

The Mission of the Sacred Heart in Cataldo, Idaho.

so passengers could enjoy refreshments there on the way from Wallace to Burke, a seven-mile trip.

On December 11, 1887, the Coeur d'Alene Railway and Navigation Company launched the steamer *Kootenai* on Lake Coeur d'Alene and the Coeur d'Alene River, providing a route from the Mission of the Sacred Heart to Coeur d'Alene City. Designed to break ice in the winter, the steamer was equipped with a 480-horsepower engine and hydraulic steering from an eight-foot screw wheel. All woodwork and machinery were done in Oregon, and the vessel was assembled on the lake.

Wallace was a rowdy town, but its residents also pitched in freely for a good cause. That happened with the town's first church. Shortly before the *Kootenai* started operations, Bishop Ethelbert Talbot, the Episcopal bishop for the territories of Idaho and Wyoming, went to Wallace to hold worship services. Before his arrival, posters carried the message, "The Bishop is coming. Let us all turn out and hear the Bishop. Services in George and Human's Hall to-morrow [*sic*], Sunday, at 11 a.m. and 8 p.m. Please leave your guns with the usher."

During the services, the bishop asked if the congregation would raise $1,000 to build a church. A Philadelphia resident, Lemuel Coffin, had already given the bishop a check for $500 on the condition that he raise the extra $1,000 to build a church in a western town. At the end of the service, the bishop happily found that about $600 was pledged.

The next day, two men asked the bishop to help them raise the rest of the money during the brief period before his train left. Within that time, they collected about $400 by cornering drinkers

The main street of Wallace, Idaho. The traffic light was the last on Interstate 90 between Seattle and Boston until September 12, 1991, when a new bypass opened. Two days later, the town held a funeral ceremony called the Last Stoplight Celebration, which drew a crowd of 1,000. There City Councilman Mike Aldredge said, "Like the whippet and the buttonhook, the iceman and the lamp lighter, the livery stable and the company store, cruel progress has eliminated the need for the services of our old friend."

in saloons.

A local minister was available to conduct services. By September 1887, the nearby town of Wardner had grown enough to have a preacher, whom the town shared with the surrounding area. As soon as Dave Cox heard the news, he celebrated by opening a saloon at the corner of Sixth and Cedar in Wallace.

As more families moved to Wallace, a school became necessary. One opened on October 19, 1887, and 15 children were expected to attend. May Peterson, a highly recommended teacher who had several years' experience on the Pacific Coast, was hired for a three-month term. Two days later, she was asked to resign. According to a newspaper report, her sudden termination resulted from "rumors... which were not calculated to raise her in the estimation of the public." One week later, the newspaper announced that Miss Peterson and George Fitzgibbons were engaged. She resumed teaching after the wedding.

Holidays were important to Wallace residents, and everyone participated in one fashion or another. Dances, games, and home-cooked meals were part of the celebrations. A turkey shoot took place outside Wallace the day before Thanksgiving 1887. The *Wallace Free Press* carried the story: "A turkey's head was the mark, 60 yards the distance, and we are told that a dozen marksmen, more or less, did the shooting. When finished, the turkey's condition was no worse than when the engagement began. As a last resort, the turkey went off at a raffle." The newspaper suggested that a rifle team be organized.

Fourth of July celebrations were the grandest. In 1888, the biggest attractions were hourly 30-foot balloon ascensions. Wallace also played a baseball game against Burke on a level field at the western end of Bank Street. The game was called in the sixth inning, with Burke leading by a score of 16 to 13. Neither bad weather nor darkness stopped the game; the town had only two baseballs and both had been lost by then.

Wallace continued to grow. On May 2, 1888, it became the first incorporated town in Shoshone County. Its population doubled to 1,000 in less than a year. By the end of 1889, it had four or five hotels, which were full most of the time. According to a *Helena Journal* reporter, the saloons operated faro games and were quite busy. The reporter described the showhouse girls as wearing abbreviated skirts to solicit drinks and smiles that drew the last quarter from unsuspecting visitors. Patrons ordered drinks "fast and furious," said the reporter, and it was necessary to go outside to get a breath of fresh air.

The town's rapid expansion resulted from increases in promising claims, richly producing mines, and new strikes. The Granite Mine declared what is believed to be the first corporate dividend by any mine in the South Fork drainage—$5,000. Other large mines in the district included the Poorman, Tiger, San Francisco, Gem, and Black Bear mines.

At that time, the Poorman shipped about 40 tons of concentrates per day. One shipment of ore netted more than $70 per ton, and the mine's stock had risen from 27 cents to $1 per share. By mid-1889, the Poorman was the largest shipping mine in the Coeur d'Alene District, with a payroll of 100 and a shaft 300 feet deep. The mine paid its shareholders $55,000 in dividends during the summer.

Shaft sinkers at the Poorman used compressed air as a power source for their drills—an innovation in those days. Men in the other mines drilled by hand. Hand drilling continued into the twentieth century, causing many miners to die prematurely of silicosis, a lung condition resulting from the dry rock dust they breathed.

Miners also used explosives underground to remove rock for processing, but they were more creative with explosives when they weren't working. They tried explosives for "fishing in a hurry," celebrating notable events, and blowing up railroad bridges, especially ahead of trains bringing federal troops into the district to regulate labor negotiations.

Labor problems brewed as the mines grew. In 1888, the towns of Burke and Wardner organized miners' unions. The first recorded dispute involved a worker at the Tiger concentrator, who was fired because he did not buy his groceries at the company store. The mine's superintendent refused to fire the man and filed his own resignation. Management would not accept it, so both men kept their jobs.

The first strike occurred on May 6, 1890, when the night shift at the Tiger Mine complained about the food at the boarding house. Management immediately fired them. The next morning, the day shift refused to go to work until the other shift was rehired. The strike continued for five days, when both shifts returned to work. No details were reported on how the matter was resolved.

By the end of 1890, tensions spread between employers and

employees. Employees wanted better wages and working conditions. Various unions throughout the district united in a Central Miners' Union, which established its headquarters in Wallace. About the same time, the Mine Owners' Association secretly organized and started a series of meetings to decide whether they would close the mines.

To further complicate matters, the railroad raised freight rates by $2 per ton, which totaled $100 per day extra for some mine owners. They responded by closing some of their mines.

When the mines reopened, members of the Mine Owners' Association said they would not hire any union members. They gave employed union workers 24 hours to withdraw their memberships or be fired.

The Coeur d'Alene Mining and Concentration Company imposed an injunction against four local unions, the Central Miners' Union, and some individuals to stop interfering. The marshal showed a copy of the injunction to Adam Aulbach, editor of the *Wallace Free Press*, and Aulbach believed he was also being served. He destroyed two pages of his next paper, which covered the labor problem.

Meanwhile, mine owners began advertising in the East for workers, while the unions placed notices discouraging replies to

Sierra Silver Mine, a former working silver mine north of Wallace that offers tours to the public.

those ads. However, 73 men came from Minnesota on a special labor train to work at the Union Mine in Burke. Almost as many men, armed with Winchesters, guarded them. Sixteen men deserted the labor train before it reached the Coeur d'Alene district, and after the train reached Burke, some of the men refused to work when they saw the labor situation. Within a week, 24 of the men had quit.

Differences reached a boiling point on July 9, 1892. During an evening of drinking, a Gem Mine guard and discharged Frisco Mine guard spoke offensive words about the union and said they were willing to fight anyone who disagreed. Some union workers took the challenge. The Gem Mine guard was almost killed, but the Frisco Mine guard escaped to spread news about the fight.

The next day, a miner went to visit a family who lived below the Gem mill. On the way, he crossed the mill property's line and a guard warned him away. A fistfight started and the miner severely beat the guard, then went home. Hundreds of people saw the fight, but no one intervened.

About 30 minutes later, three Gem guards rushed up the canyon to the miner's house, but some union men grabbed their guns and chased them. Not wanting trouble, the guards hurried to the Frisco Mine.

Little did the men know that a war was about to begin. A warrant was issued for the miners' arrest on charges of assault with a deadly weapon. Armed union men from Wallace, Mullan, and Burke began gathering at the Gem Mine.

The next morning, men at the Frisco Mine saw groups of armed men on both sides of the canyon overlooking the mine. At about 5 a.m., the union men opened fire. The guards believed the shots were intended to scare them away, but when the bullets came closer, the guards took cover in the mill and returned fire.

Some union men decided to circle the canyon and come out above the mill. They reached a sidehill tramway, loaded a car with powder boxes, and sent the load with a lit fuse down a water flume into the mill. The fuse was short, so the powder exploded sooner than the men had hoped, but it destroyed the tracks. Then the men went to the flume and dropped powder down the penstock to the mill. The explosions destroyed the building, killing one man and injuring several others. Damage was estimated at $20,000.

While the explosions took place, the shooting continued. The

Frisco guards discovered they were outnumbered and surrendered.

Another fight started the same day at the Gem Mine while the day shift relieved the night shift. Shots poured into the town of Gem. Women and children escaped to other nearby towns. The sheriff and federal marshal arrived and called a truce.

On July 13, Governor Norman B. Willey proclaimed Shoshone County in a state of rebellion and ordered troops stationed in Wallace, Wardner, Mullan, and Gem. They arrested the troublemakers, and more troops received orders to stand by in case they were needed. The area remained under martial law until November 19, 1892.

During the dispute, workers lost more than $1 million in wages and the mines suffered tremendous losses. The railroads also lost about $1 million in freight charges.

The labor disputes did not seem to affect Wallace's population. Neither did a devastating fire.

On July 27, 1890, a deflective flue in the Central Hotel caught on fire. The flames spread in the dry summer heat and destroyed Wallace's business district. Most of the homes were spared.

The Northern Pacific Railroad Depot, now a historical museum. In 1986, the depot was moved 200 feet south of its original location to make room for the Interstate 90 bypass that opened on September 12, 1991.

Despite the damage, the town merchants were optimistic. Before the flames were extinguished, some merchants were running for the telegraph to wire orders for replacement supplies. They opened tent stores until they could rebuild. Even the next issue of the newspaper was printed on scorched paper.

Brick buildings replaced wooden structures in the business district, and by February 1891, Wallace had 30 saloons, three owned by women. Two gambling establishments were also operating.

Unlike most mining towns, Wallace did not die because of shrinking mineral supplies. By the 1930s, the district was one of the top mining regions in the world, making Idaho the leading state in the country in silver production, and second in lead production.

Wallace remains a mining town today. Sagging silver prices in the 1980s closed several mines and kept the population at about 1,000. Despite the decline, the Coeur d'Alene Mining District is still the world's leading silver producer. The top producing silver mines in the United States are there, and some operations are conducted more than 3,000 feet below sea level. The district is also the all-time leader in silver production. Approximately one billion ounces have been removed since Colonel Wallace settled there in 1884.

The Old West spirit has not left the town, either. Hardy, independent residents share a camaraderie that only those living in a hardrock mining town can understand. It is a characteristic that will last for years to come.

Washington Territory's Matchmaker

Seattle, Washington

In the nineteenth century, most people rarely changed careers. They chose an occupation to support their families and stayed with it for life.

But others tried a variety of jobs. They moved from one town to another and enjoyed some brief periods of success.

Asa Mercer was among them. He switched careers as if he were a cat with nine lives. In his 78-year life span, he was a carpenter, university president, legislator, businessman, publisher, editor, and writer. He even managed to get involved in Wyoming's Johnson County War, probably one of the nastiest range wars in U.S. history. But the most ambitious of his brief pursuits—and probably the most unusual—was recruiting single women from the East Coast to wed the lonely male inhabitants of the fledgling Washington Territory.

In the 1860s, few women lived in the Pacific Northwest. In the Seattle area, men outnumbered them nine to one. Mercer became aware of this imbalance when he moved there from Ohio in 1861, fresh out of Franklin College.

While working as a carpenter at the newly chartered territorial university (now the University of Washington), he was promoted to president. At the time, there were no students. Mercer met this challenge head-on by scouring the

countryside and logging camps, recruiting students with the zeal of a big-time, modern college football coach. The settlers were interested but unwilling to leave their only sources of income. Mercer solved this problem by arranging Saturday work, logging all day at $1.50 a cord, and accumulated 15 to 20 students for his first class.

While Mercer possessed a flair for promotion, he didn't realize his students would also give him an education. He had much to learn about life in the Northwest. As the first few terms at the university flew by, he discovered that obtaining a higher education was not the highest of his students' priorities. They sought female companionship.

Desperate to keep enrollment up, the quick-thinking Mercer decided to try an ambitious idea: he would go East and return with single women ready for married life. Mercer sailed for Massachusetts in late 1863 and found 11 New England ladies with the pioneering spirit. Nine of the women made the Northwest their permanent home, one died, and another returned to the East. The settlers were so grateful to Mercer that they elected him to the territorial legislature in 1864.

Mercer attempted to expand his East Coast recruitment. On his next trip, he planned to return with several hundred women. To enhance his efforts, he wrote a pamphlet presenting Washington as a disease-free utopia. He neglected to mention the cold, rainy winters characteristic of western Washington, which some dislike more than snow, and only hinted at his motive.

He wrote, "The beauties of the climate, the vast extent of grazing lands—seven million acres of agricultural land of the finest quality—fish in a thousand bays and banks; big trees; piles and spars on hillside and plain; coal in measureless quantities beneath the hills; broad and magnificent rivers; manufacturing resources on every hand; an inland sea, and bays whitened by the sails of every nation; not one of these alone, but all announce the future of the north-west division of the United States of America...The fascinating beauty of the mountain scenery, the wild magnificence of the tumbling cataracts, and lakes of placid beauty, add much to the bulk of attraction.

"Over twenty thousand farms lie within our borders, upon which families can locate, and by efficient effort make the 'wilderness blossom as the rose.' The citizens of the Territory are generally an intelligent people, and all that is lacking to make comfort dwell in the shadow of each household, is an increase of population, and especially the introduction of female society in greater abundance."

Mercer sought financial aid from the Washington legislature. They gave him plenty of moral support but not a single penny. The desperate male settlers, however, were willing to help as much as possible—even when it meant forking over as much as $300 apiece to cover Mercer's expenses. Many others entrusted him with hard-earned savings to purchase agricultural equipment and other supplies.

Unfortunately, the pioneers' contributions could not completely finance this ambitious endeavor, so Mercer decided to go to Washington, DC, and look up his "old friend," President Abraham Lincoln. As a child in the Midwest, Mercer had sat on Abe's lap. But he didn't know Lincoln was assassinated until after he arrived on the East Coast in 1865. Saddened but still carrying high hopes, Mercer proceeded to badger every government official he could corner, starting with President Andrew Johnson. All were sympathetic but not interested.

Finally, he found a friend in General Ulysses S. Grant, who, after four years on the war front, understood male loneliness. Grant signed for use of the *Continental*, an old Civil War ship, to transport the women back to the Northwest, but the quartermaster refused to issue the vessel. Instead, he offered to sell the *Continental* to Mercer for $80,000, one-third of its worth but well beyond Mercer's means.

Soon a shrewd businessman caught wind of Mercer's plight and stepped forward with his own deal. He bought the ship and offered

A view of Lower Manhattan in New York City from the Staten Island Ferry. The Brooklyn Bridge is on the right. When Asa Mercer arrived here in 1865 to recruit brides to the Pacific Northwest, New Yorkers' responses to his venture were mixed.

cut-rate fares. There was one catch: if fewer than 200 passengers signed on, full fare would be charged. Mercer, much relieved, readily agreed and headed off to New York City to fill his roster.

New Yorkers responded with mixed opinions, and the financial delay in securing transportation was a great disadvantage. *The New York Tribune* hailed his noble efforts, while *The New York Herald* claimed the west-bound women would become inmates of brothels serving a pack of lecherous louts. As a result, many originally enthusiastic supporters canceled, leaving Mercer with only 46 eligible women and Civil War widows. Others who planned to go despite the media's criticisms canceled when they could not afford the fee for their passage ($50 down, $25 upon arrival in Seattle).

For those who boarded the ship, the trip to Seattle was far from peaceful. On the second day of the voyage, one of the women lost her false teeth overboard during a bout with seasickness and had to choke down the daily diet of parboiled beans, fried salt pork, and tea steeped in salt water for the next three months. While the ship sailed from New York around Cape Horn, it was caught in the crossfire of a battle between Spain and Chile. A crew member drowned after he was helped overboard by another crew member. And one woman, who felt an arm go around her waist as she sat knitting, plunged a needle halfway into the offending limb.

Mercer discovered quickly that his so-called "fragile" cargo really consisted of extremely strong-willed, independent individuals, and he faced difficulties in preventing them from flirting with the ship's crew, especially the officers. Roger Conant, a reporter for *The New York Times*, sailed with the group and observed one of Mercer's attempts to distract them. According to Conant's journals, Mercer invented games to keep the women occupied for hours. One was guessing proverbs, or "spiritual rappings," from the Bible. Another was called—appropriately enough—the Continental Game. "He would take a pack of cards, and writing a subject upon them, would distribute them face down to those engaged in the play," wrote Conant. "The first in order reverses the card, rises and immediately proceeds to speak for five minutes on the subject which fate has assigned him. The play took amazingly certain [*sic*] with certain old Maiden Members of the party, but the young and gay couldn't see the joke, and flirted with the officers harder than ever."

By the time the *Continental* reached San Francisco on April 25,

1866, five of the passengers were already engaged, including one to Mercer. Five others continued circling around an eligible California miner and became known as the Constellation.

Mercer arrived in San Francisco with $3 in his pocket, so he cabled Governor William Pickering in Washington for help. All he received was a $7.50 cable, collect, offering regrets. To finish the trip, Mercer sold the agricultural equipment.

Mercer's problems were not over. More rumors from San Franciscans about the weather and the undesirable personalities of the Northwest settlers prevented about half of Mercer's cargo from continuing the trip. The rest found themselves drifting on lumber boats for the last leg of their journey.

By the time they reached Seattle, Mercer's greatly magnified money problems turned out to be the least of his worries. A horde of female-starved backwoodsmen had somehow concluded they were entitled to claim the women like baggage, then march uptown to the justice of the peace. They descended upon the lumber vessel like vultures. But Mercer, unintimidated, stood his ground. Love in Seattle, he proclaimed, would be earned.

Needless to say, Washingtonians greeted Mercer with considerably less enthusiasm on his second return from New York. Most, however, understood—although they may not have forgiven—after Mercer gave several required public explanations, one of which was published in the *Puget Sound Weekly* newspaper.

Even if Mercer gave in to the settlers' demands, the women passengers would have intervened. They wanted to choose their own mates, and they expressed their intentions firmly. According to Conant's journal, they openly refused to marry anyone who contracted with Mercer and "wouldn't even speak to them."

Some of the women wed quickly while many others spent more time looking. According to the periodical *Social Verses*, all but "two or three" of them were attached by 1869.

Conant wrote that one old woodsman met the widow "W" (presumably Sarah Wakeman) at 3 p.m., offered his hand at 6 p.m., and was accepted at 9 p.m.

Forty-year-old Mary Martin married a 25-year-old oiler who worked on the *Continental.* A Mrs. Horton, age 70, also found a mate shortly after she arrived. Ida May Barlow Pinkham, a 20-year-old linguist, married the man who carried her bags from the lumber vessel to the hotel. They had 14 children.

Ann Conner, age 40, married Mark Hattsuck after teaching for three years in Olympia. In a letter home, she complained about the food, lack of privacy, rough seas, and brazen flirting on the journey west, but added, "I did not regret my moving and try [*sic*] to support myself."

One of the ladies married exceptionally well. Elizabeth Peebles came west with her sister, Anna, strictly to see the country. They did not intend to stay and did not consider themselves among the fruits of Mercer's promotional efforts. Elizabeth taught school in Olympia and was the first woman clerk of the legislature before marrying Angus MacKintosh in 1871. Angus was said to be worth $100,000 by some sources. The couple's son, Kenneth, became a judge. Anna became deputy collector of internal revenue in Olympia before she wed Amos Brown in 1867. Her salary was $75 per month.

The unwelcome circumstances surrounding Mercer's return to Seattle sent a strong message—it was time to move on. So he headed to Oregon in 1866, where he continued working to foster trade with the East and encourage immigration. The governor soon appointed him to commissioner for immigration. Mercer continued his promotional pursuits by writing pamphlets lauding his new state.

A view of downtown Seattle from Kerry Park on Queen Anne Hill.

He also began a career in journalism by establishing *The Oregon Grange* newspaper.

Eight years later, the urge to wander hit Mercer again. He moved to Texas, where he ran four different newspapers during the next decade. While he was there, he also became an expert on the cattle industry. In 1886, the State of California commissioned him to study and analyze its growing cattle business.

Mercer moved to Cheyenne, Wyoming, before the State of California hired him to complete the study. With his involvement in the Johnson County War, he wore out his welcome again. This time, he did not leave. Instead, he confined himself to a 900-acre farm.

While details on the rest of his life are sketchy, it appears that time eventually healed most wounds. By 1906, he was writing pamphlets boosting Wyoming, and he began working as a tour guide at Yellowstone National Park.

Mercer died in 1917 at the age of 78. Although he worked at nearly two dozen occupations during his lifetime, he never tried to write an autobiography, which is why he probably remains an energetic and engaging, yet highly elusive figure, in the development of the West.

Today, feelings in Seattle have mellowed toward the well-intentioned man who tried to recruit brides to the Pacific Northwest more than a century ago. A major traffic artery in downtown Seattle and an island nearby in Lake Washington share his last name. Mercer Island is aptly named; its shape, a footprint, is a symbolic reminder of the matchmaker who was not afraid to take the first step to aid the region's growth.

Women are in Charge Here

Jacksonville, Oregon

Pioneer women stopping a war? It happened in Jacksonville, Oregon, during the 1850s. Many of their miner husbands welcomed the excitement of the Rogue Indian War, a struggle between the new settlers and the Shasta, Takelma, and Athapascan nations over land rights, and enthusiastically joined the volunteer companies who fought the Indians. The women, however, took a dim view of their spouses' leaving them unprotected.

So, they held a secret meeting in the church and vowed to withhold the "expectations of home life" until the men saw the error of their ways. Naturally, the men soon surrendered, but not without briefly retaliating by hoisting a petticoat on the town's flagpole.

Colorful, lively incidents like these peppered the pioneers' daily life in Jacksonville during its years as a mining boom town and center of commerce in southern Oregon.

In the 1840s and 1850s, seemingly endless streams of mule trains, carrying groceries, clothing, and tools, followed the trails from Portland, Oregon, to the goldfields of northern California. Often the mules grazed in the valley north of the Siskiyou Mountains before beginning the slow climb across the steep range.

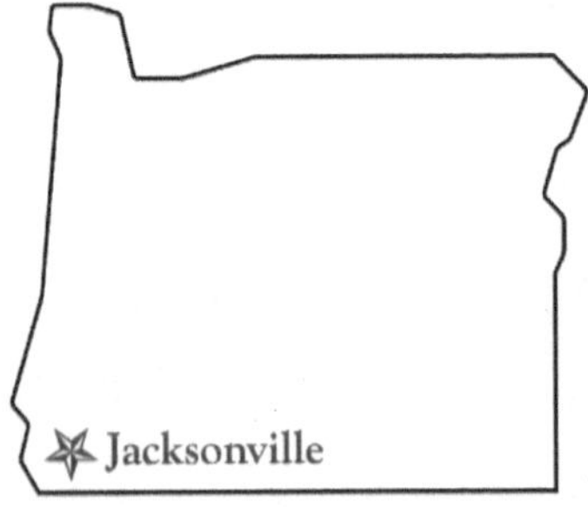

On a rainy December morning in 1852, James Cluggage and James Poole, two packers rounding up their mules at Rich Gulch Creek to continue their journey to the

The Jacksonville Tavern, or "J'ville Tavern" for short, on Jacksonville's main street. It's the oldest tavern in the Rogue River Valley.

mines in Yreka, California, saw something shining in the mule track. When they looked closer, they noticed it was gold. They applied for and received a Donation Land Claim, and platted a town in the southwest corner of the property.

Word of the discovery spread like wildfire, and fortune seekers flooded the area. Within weeks, every foot of the surrounding hills and gullies were staked, and prospectors reported huge finds every day.

The log and tent city that mushroomed overnight was named Table Rock City after a nearby mesa, but when the state established Jackson County on January 12, 1852, most settlers adopted the name Jacksonville. The population swelled to about 1,000.

Over time, framed and brick structures replaced tents and log cabins, and Jacksonville developed into a financial and trading center in the vast wilderness separating San Francisco and Portland. Wells Fargo stages connected Jacksonville with the two cities on the nation's second longest stage route—1,100 miles of rugged traveling. The stages hauled away bags of gold dust and returned with colorful characters lured by their dreams of becoming rich.

Jacksonville's gold deposits, found underground and in neighboring rivers and streams, were by far the richest in Oregon. In 1856, the peak year of the gold rush, almost $1.5 million crossed the counter at Beekman Bank, founded and owned by Cornelius C. Beekman.

Interesting stories emerge in gold rush towns like Jacksonville. One of the most memorable is of two men who were confined in the town's jail. The jailer was more interested in digging in his nearby claim than promptly feeding the prisoners, so the two men decided to escape by digging a tunnel through the dirt floor of their cell. Instead, they struck a rich vein of gold, so they decided it was okay to miss a few meals.

Naturally, when the inmates' sentences ended, they were reluctant to leave, which caused the unsuspecting jailer to scratch his head in wonder.

Saloon stories are as unforgettable. One miner refused to be taunted into buying drinks for the saloon crowd. Finally, when someone accused him of being stingy, he angrily waved his poke containing $700 in gold dust and yelled, "By God, I'll show you how stingy I am!" He dashed outside the saloon and scattered the gold dust on the street.

Another story recalls a miner who was down to his last speck of gold dust. Nevertheless, he told the bartender, "Set 'em up." While the crowd was served, he rushed out to dig up enough gold to pay for the round and returned as the last customer received his drink.

Then there was the biggest event Jacksonville had ever seen—the overnight visit of Republican President Rutherford B. Hayes on September 27, 1880. When the stage stopped that evening on the main street, the President and his eight-member party, exhausted from the tough ride over the mountains, descended stiffly from the coach to await whatever hospitality the town would offer.

Disorganization and haste described the arrangements. Because there was no advance notice of exactly when these dignitaries would arrive, the welcoming committee didn't show up. Neither did the mayor. Instead, a booming cannon and brass band greeted the group.

No earlier plans were made for overnight accommodations for the President's party, either. Madame Jeanne Holt was summoned to board everyone in her new United States Hotel, but there was a problem—no rooms were ready.

The hotel was under construction, had no furniture, and the paint was still fresh and sticky. The only part of the hotel in some sort of presentable fashion was the upstairs ballroom, where the town held a Fourth of July dance two months earlier.

Citizens quickly planned and scheduled a reception and dinner in the ballroom, while Madame Holt frantically borrowed furniture for the guests' sleeping quarters. Cornelius C. Beekman, Jacksonville's leading Republican and the town's only banker, was asked to give a welcoming speech at the banquet. Lucie Webb Hayes, the President's wife who was known as "Lemonade Lucy" for her prohibitionist activities, would be the keynote speaker.

But Mrs. Hayes wouldn't address the audience of miners, farmers, and businessmen who attended the banquet. She turned her wine glass upside down as a gesture of refusal. The local ladies were so intrigued by this genuine bit of Washington etiquette that it became a custom.

The United States Hotel, where President Rutherford B. Hayes and his wife, Lucy Webb Hayes, overnighted on September 27, 1880. Hotel owner Jeanne Holt tried to charge President Hayes and his party $100 for the accommodations at a time when the most expensive room at an exclusive hotel in San Francisco was $6 per night.

The next morning, Madame Holt presented General William T. Sherman, a member of the party, a bill for $100 (at a time when the nicest room at San Francisco's best hotel, the Palace, was $6 a night).

General Sherman stared at the bill, then snapped, "My dear lady, I did not intend to buy your hotel!"

A brief dispute followed, and two versions exist of the outcome. The first claims General Sherman paid in full. In the other, he paid only a portion of the bill, which prompted Madame Holt to write numerous letters to Washington. Sources don't indicate whether she received the rest of the money.

Generally, most of the women living in mining towns were dance hall girls, but in Jacksonville, many were the wives of hardworking miners. As the female population increased, so did the need for a church. True to the spirit of the American pioneer woman, a group of determined wives—the same ones who stopped their husbands from fighting in the Rogue Indian War—bravely entered each saloon and gambling house to solicit funds. The miners and gamblers, greatly embarrassed by their invasion of their male sanctuaries, contributed generously. The women collected enough yellow dust to build a Methodist church. It was the first Protestant church west of the Rocky Mountains.

In 1856, the population of Jacksonville shrunk as the easy ore and dust supplies declined. The town remained the center of commerce for southern Oregon until two major blows occurred—the building of the railroad through Medford, five miles east, in the 1880s, and the county seat moving to Medford in 1927.

But before the town had a chance to fade away, it attracted national attention. In 1923, the DeAutremont brothers (Ray, Roy, and Hugh) held up a Southern Pacific train in a tunnel high in the Siskiyou Mountains. They believed there was money in the mail car, but before their theory was disproven, they had killed the railway mail clerk and three other trainmen.

Police thoroughly searched the area but couldn't find any trace of the three brothers. They weren't captured until four years later, thanks to more than 2.5 million wanted posters distributed worldwide. Two were caught in Ohio; the other was serving in the Philippines when a fellow soldier recognized him. The men were returned to Jackson County, and Judge C.M. Thomas sentenced them to life in the Oregon State Penitentiary. It was the last trial in the courthouse.

Jacksonville's main street.

After the trial ended, Jacksonville practically became a ghost town. A few dedicated citizens stayed and decided to preserve its heritage. They managed to keep many of the small frame cottages and brick commercial buildings dating from the town's founding. The courthouse was restored and opened as a museum on July 10, 1950. In the early 1960s, residents restored the downtown core with federal urban renewal funds, and by 1967, the town received the first National Historic Landmark District designation in the West.

Today, Jacksonville is a comfortable town of about 2,900 people, more than double the population during its heyday. Tourists are now its primary industry. The Britt Pavilion attracts top-name acts ranging from the Goo Goo Dolls to ZZ Top. The venue is on the estate of Peter Britt, an immigrant from Switzerland and professional photographer who documented the history of the Rogue River Valley for more than 50 years. The home of Cornelius Beekman and his historic bank are open for tours. Popular annual events include Haunted History in October and Victorian Christmas in December.

Some restored homes have been turned into antique shops, which are great places to see the types of furniture, clothing, tools, and cooking ware used in pioneer times.

Jacksonville's setting has also attracted movie producers. In 1970, Universal Studios filmed *The Great Northfield, Minnesota Raid*, the story of 10 savage minutes when the notorious James-Younger Gang unsuccessfully attempted to hold up the Northfield First National Bank on September 7, 1876. All the producers needed to do to lend authentic flavor to the movie was to remove the telephone poles from the main street, cover the pavement with an inch or so of dirt, and lay boardwalks over the sidewalks.

Wool Capital of the World

Shaniko, Oregon

Unlike many Old West towns, Shaniko, Oregon, didn't spring into existence from a vast gold strike. Wool was its lifeblood.

In the mid-1800s, the high desert of southern Wasco County was a vast, quiet land full of bunch grass, sagebrush, and rocks. A gold rush in Canyon City broke the silence in 1862 when thousands of miners walked or rode horses through isolated country to reach the new settlement about 190 miles southeast of The Dalles.

Traveling to Canyon City was difficult, even on horseback. No roads existed, so pack trains carried supplies. Pack train operators risked their lives taking necessities to the miners and hauling gold back to The Dalles. During their trips, they encountered robberies from bandits and Indian attacks.

The constant threats sparked complaints that finally reached Washington, DC. In February 1867, the State of Oregon received a grant to build a military wagon road from The Dalles to Fort Boise, Idaho. After the road was finished, settlers began homesteading between The Dalles and Canyon City. By the time the gold rush ended, they had established a strong sheep-ranching community. Sheep were an ideal choice for central Oregon because they could traverse uneven and rocky terrain easily and did not tire quickly.

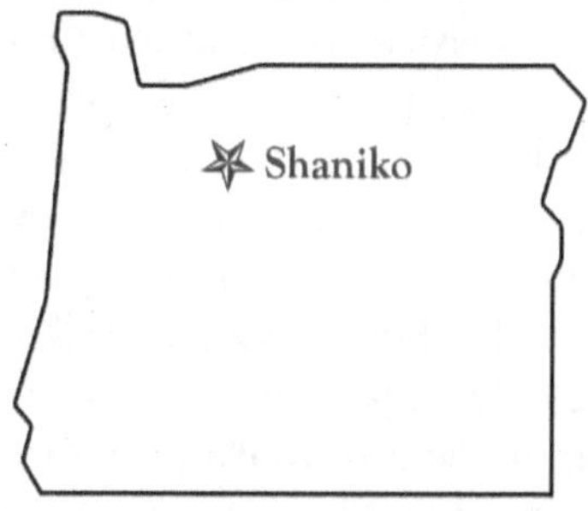

Sheep ranchers transported their wool to The Dalles, the only market in the region. One delivery

The Shaniko School.

often meant traveling more than 200 miles round-trip.

To make shipping more convenient, some bankers and businessmen invested funds in 1898 to build the Columbia Southern Railway at Biggs Junction. The developers chose Cross Hollows, a former stagecoach stop, as the terminus for the line and bought a section of land on a hill overlooking the old station. They plotted streets for a town and installed a water system. Ranchers were so enthusiastic about the new railroad that they worked their own teams and scoops during the two-year project. And when businessman J.J. Wiley heard the railroad would end in Shaniko, he quickly built a saloon to serve the anticipated flood of settlers and traders.

Cross Hollows' name was changed to Shaniko in honor of August Scherneckau, the former stagecoach stop keeper and postmaster. The Indians nicknamed him "Shaniko" because they couldn't pronounce his last name. While living in Cross Hollows, Scherneckau contributed greatly to the town's prosperity by building a store, a saloon, and a 16-room inn that generated up to $50,000 each year during the Canyon City gold rush.

Within a year, Shaniko transformed from a tent camp of construction workers into a trade center, where horse-drawn wagon trains hauled wool and wheat into town and carried supplies to small communities scattered over a 20,000-square-mile area. Shaniko

Warehouse, the largest wool and wheat warehouse in the state, was finished that year. Its capacity was four million pounds of wool and any amount of wheat that arrived there. A second warehouse measuring 75,000 square feet followed, along with other buildings to store hay, coal, barley, and kerosene.

Shaniko became the "wool capital of the world." Population estimates range from about 800 to 1,500 during the boom years. People from as far away as San Francisco and Boston attended the large wool sales. The streets, hotel, and saloons were crowded with buyers, salesmen who advertised their wares, and curious visitors.

Freighters brought large bags of wool into town on rigs of three or four wagons behind four- to six-horse teams. Empty wagons and teams stayed overnight at the wagon yard, an enclosed space near the houses of pleasure, which was owned by the only woman in Shaniko bold enough to smoke a cigarette in public.

In the spring, ranchers who lived closer to Shaniko herded their sheep to the shearing yards at the west side of town to remove the wool. Each shearer had their own pen.

The Shaniko City Hall.

As many as three wool sales were scheduled every year in Shaniko. A private railroad Pullman car took buyers to town the night before each sale to give them a full day to examine and bid on the wool they wanted.

On the day of the sale, a warehouseman pulled down a sack from the top of each wool-owner's pile and slit it open. Buyers removed a fleece, separated a handful of wool, and examined it for texture, shrinkage, and staple. ("Staple" refers to the length and fineness of each lock or tuft of wool.) They then placed sealed bids on the wool they wanted. The warehouse foreman received the bids and brought them to the owner of the wool. Then they discussed each bid to determine whether any were acceptable. If the owner agreed to a price, he received a check from the customer. Then the owner settled his accounts in town, which usually included a stop for refreshments at a saloon, and returned to his ranch.

When the sale ended, the buyers left Shaniko. The wool remained behind to be baled, marked, and loaded into boxcars for shipping.

As the wool market expanded, so did the railroad. By 1902, Shaniko had maintenance shops to repair equipment and keep the engines running smoothly. Branch offices representing the Columbia Southern Railway opened in Moro and Portland.

The Shaniko Bank.

The Shaniko Gage Museum.

Despite Shaniko's overwhelming progress, other forces were causing declines of the town and the railroad. In 1911, a rival railroad completed a line along Deschutes Canyon, connecting routes into California. Small communities that formerly used the terminal at Shaniko now had direct access to their own railroad. Later that year, a fire swept through Shaniko's business district, destroying most of the buildings. None were rebuilt.

The Columbia Southern Railway continued to ship carloads of wool, wheat, and livestock from Shaniko, but not enough to keep the town alive. By 1959, Shaniko was declared a ghost town, and five years later, the railroad closed after melting snow from an unusually heavy snowfall washed out the line in Biggs Canyon.

For decades, Shaniko's wooden sidewalks led to emptiness. Then in 2000, Robert B. Pamplin Jr. bought the Shaniko Hotel and some small businesses and city lots. He renovated some of the buildings and planned to build homes for workers he hired to serve the tourists. When he applied for an easement to supply water from one of his lots to the hotel and restaurant, the Shaniko City Council denied it. Pamplin closed the hotel and restaurant, capped the well, and listed the property for sale.

Several years later, David Long, a Shaniko resident, raised money to renovate the hotel through the South Wasco Fire and Rescue Association and reopened it in August 2023. Other buildings are being or have been restored, and more businesses are in operation. A general store on U.S. Highway 97, the main road through town, sells groceries and other staples. Most businesses are open April through September. Thirty-two people live there year-round.

Annual events include the Hoot, Holler, and Sing Bluegrass Campout on Memorial Day weekend; the Shaniko Ragtime & Vintage Music Festival on the first weekend in October; and Shaniko Days on the first weekend in August. Shaniko Days features artisans selling their products, food vendors, live music, a cake auction, stand-up comedy, gunfight shows, and a church service.

The general store on U.S. Highway 97 in Shaniko.

Yukon Food Drive

Various Points in Alaska and Dawson City, Yukon

At the height of the Klondike Gold Rush in July 1897, the Reverend Sheldon Jackson, the first agent of the U.S. Bureau of Education in Alaska, traveled from Teller Station on the Seward Peninsula to Dawson City, Yukon. When he returned to Teller Station, a rumor that famine would strike started in Alaska and spread to the lower United States.

The story predicted an estimated 4,000 to 5,000 prospectors in Dawson City and Circle City might starve before the next winter ended because the Yukon River, the main supply route, would be useless after it froze. Who started the rumor remains uncertain, but most sources attribute it to Jackson. Regardless, Jackson believed

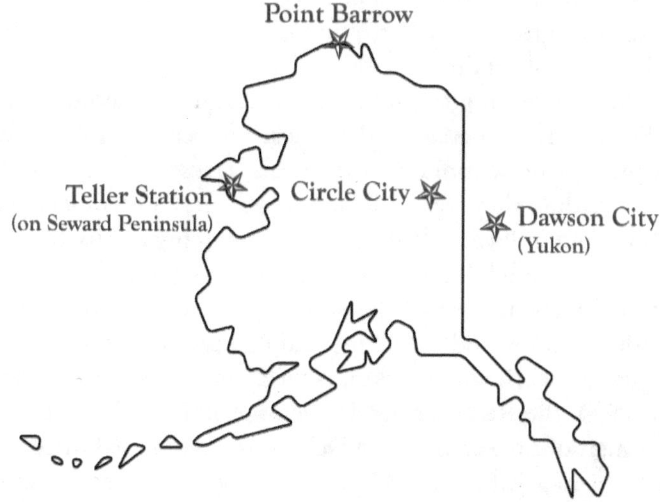

impending starvation was a real problem, and he asked Congress for money to deliver freight from the Alaska coast to the Yukon using harness-broken reindeer imported from Scandinavia.

In December 1897, Congress passed a bill giving the War Department $200,000 to accomplish the task. Secretary of War Russell Alger asked Jackson to purchase 500 reindeer, sleds, reindeer moss, and harnesses. Two hundred head would be given to the War Department in Alaska for surveying and scientific studies, and the miners would receive the remaining three hundred. Alger also wanted Jackson to go to Norway and hire drivers to care for the herd.

Jackson was no stranger to coordinating reindeer drives, but his earlier efforts were on a much smaller scale. His interest started as a guest aboard the Coast Guard cutter *Bear* in 1890, when he overheard officers mention the Alaskan Eskimos were starving from a lack of game. Arctic whaling fleets were rapidly killing whales and walruses and introducing whiskey and disease. The Eskimos' other food sources, wild reindeer and caribou, were wiped out by the Caucasian settlers.

The conversation gave Jackson an idea. He would import deer from Siberia and teach the Eskimos how to raise them. To fund the project, he asked for help from Congress. Congress wouldn't approve the money, so Jackson solicited private subscriptions. By the summer of 1891, he raised $2,150, which he used to buy 20 deer, hire Siberian herders, and begin training. Eskimos who successfully completed the five-year program received their own herds. Then in 1892, Congress decided the project was successful and began providing annual funding.

As the operation grew, Jackson found it harder to buy reindeer from Siberia. The Siberians did not want to sell live animals when they could get more money for the skins. Jackson's trainers did not work out, either; they were sullen, disobedient, and temperamental. One moody employee killed a deer by stamping on its head. The problems prompted Jackson to write a correspondent, "It is our intention to try to secure the services of several young married Laplanders, who would be willing and competent to take charge of the herds and teach young Eskimos their care and management."

In 1893, the Reindeer Service became an official agency of the Department of the Interior, and Jackson was appointed director. He hired William Kjellman, a 37-year-old Norwegian immigrant and naturalized American citizen, to work as an agent in Scandinavia. Before he was hired, Kjellman had been a herder and reindeer-supply salesman who knew Norwegian, Finnish, English, and Lapp dialects.

When Congress passed the 1897 bill to provide food to the Yukon miners, Kjellman was already in Norway. Jackson asked him to buy supplies and hire herders as quickly as possible. The task would not be easy. The most difficult challenge was finding men willing to travel to a new, unfamiliar land. As a result, Kjellman made some concessions. Some potential employees accepted his offer on the condition they could marry their sweethearts and take them to Alaska. Those who were already married wanted to bring their wives and children. Personal bills had to be paid because the herders would probably be gone for a very long time—possibly a lifetime. The ensuing farewell parties seemed endless.

When all the arrangements were settled, preparations for the journey began. The herders put 538 deer, sleds, harnesses, and 250 tons of moss into a warehouse near the village of Trondjeim, Norway, and waited for the steamer *Manitoban* to arrive.

The *Manitoban* had to be anchored offshore because it could not be tied to the tiny dock in such shallow water. Barges carried the supplies, deer, and passengers to the ship. The barges were so small that only one deer could be moved at a time. The herders worked as longshoremen from early morning until after seven o'clock that night with only one break, a brief lunch. By night, they were too tired to continue. The next morning they returned to work, and by dinnertime, everything was loaded, including the passengers—72

Ellis Island in New York City, where the herders were rushed through immigration upon their arrival to the United States. From 1892 through 1924, more than 20 million immigrants passed through here.

men, 19 women, and 26 children.

At four o'clock the next morning, February 4, 1898, the vessel got underway. For the next 23 days, passengers endured crowded, uncomfortable conditions. Rain and snow forced them into their quarters, a poorly lit room in the bottom deck's steerage area used for sleeping, cooking, and eating. Most of the deer stayed on the upper deck and the continuous precipitation caused urine and dung to leak into the lower two decks. Children fearing the dark and parents worrying about uncertain futures became violently seasick. One of the herders, Carl Sacariasen, kept a diary of the voyage and wrote that the sounds and odors were too much for him. He slept with the deer despite the bad weather.

When the vessel arrived in New York City, the passengers were rushed through immigration and loaded onto trains to Seattle. By the time the trains reached Ohio, Secretary of War Alger had learned that the Yukon miners were never in danger of starving. But because the project had progressed so far, he could not stop it.

Meanwhile, the herders became celebrities. Newspapers reported on the cross-country trip, and curious crowds waited at the train stations to greet them. When the trains stopped for the night and one of the herders stepped outside to look around, he was generally overcome by the friendly mob. Spectators climbed on boxes to peep into the sleeping cars.

During the trip, Sacariasen wrote that the American women were "nervy" and "forward." Some tried to take pieces of clothing, especially the long-tasseled Lapp caps. Others pushed calling cards into the herders' hands or tried to cut locks of their blond hair.

Despite Sacariasen's complaints, the men enjoyed the attention, but they were also frustrated because they could not understand English. That changed when they arrived in Seattle. People of Norwegian descent from Ballard, a community north of downtown Seattle, could talk to them. One of them, Hedly Redmyer, could also speak Finnish, which the Lapps understood. Redmyer was hired to join the herders on the rest of the journey.

While the herders waited at their Woodland Park camp for a ship to take them to Alaska, more problems developed. The War Department placed Major W.R. Abercrombie in charge of the expedition. He knew nothing about caring for deer and would not allow Kjellman to give him advice. Abercrombie assumed the deer would eat the grass in Woodland Park, so he sent the moss to storage and ordered the herders to let the deer graze. The deer did not like the grass and refused to eat it. The layover in Seattle lasted longer than expected, because Abercrombie did not charter a ship.

Frustrated by the major's command, Kjellman resigned. When the Secretary of the Interior dismissed Abercrombie and replaced him with Jackson, Kjellman reconsidered. Jackson immediately chartered the ship, *Seminole*, which left for Alaska on March 17, 1898. The tugboat *Sea Lion* towed the *Seminole* all the way from Seattle to Haines.

When the *Seminole* docked in Haines 10 days later, Army officials had not received any orders and did not know the reindeer and herders were coming. The Army's inability to make quick decisions, along with delays caused by bad weather, were disastrous. On March 29, the spring thaw began, preventing the herders from driving the animals over the ice. No moss was left, and the reindeer were starving.

Jackson stepped in again. He sent the women and children to a mission on the coast of the Bering Sea and told the men to start moving all the reindeer to Circle City. By then, however, the deer were weak and some began dying. More died on the trail.

The soft snow, still five to six feet deep in many spots, made travel difficult, but Kjellman and his men managed to find a crag where the deer could eat moss off the trees. But there was not enough food for the deer to regain much strength, and more died. The Army still had not decided whether they wanted to keep their 200 animals, so Kjellman returned to Haines Mission to press the matter. The Army did not respond, but Kjellman did receive permission to cut the number of herders to two Norwegians and 12 Lapps. Provisions would last longer with a smaller group.

On April 8, Kjellman hired eight Indians to carry supplies 20 miles up the Chilkat River while the herders drove the reindeer into the mountains. In a letter to the editor of the Norwegian publication, *Skandinaven*, dated June 5, 1899, Redmyer recalled the experience:

"Well, this was a fine expedition! The reindeer were in such poor condition that they could not walk; and it rained every day—the snow would soon disappear. It didn't look promising to set out on the journey. Finally we got all our things to the foot of a high mountain on which the reindeer were grazing....On the 12th of May we began to carry our things up (the reindeer were still too weak to pack supplies). We had a hundred pounds on our backs, and with that load we were to ascend a mountain eight or ten thousand feet high. On the 15th of May I counted the reindeer and found only 164 alive. Many had died on the mountain from sickness, caused by hunger."

About a month later, the surviving deer had regained enough strength to carry packs. Forty-five animals were needed, and after the herders caught them, "the fun began," Redmyer wrote. "I have never seen such a dance as the Lapps and the reindeer had, when the reindeer got its pack on."

In July, the herders spent more time chasing the reindeer than keeping them on the trail because the animals preferred the glaciers over the summer heat. As soon as the temperatures cooled, the herders drove the deer along the Dalton Trail to the Mendenhall River. They bought more supplies at Dalton Post and continued following the trail, "for it had become much colder and besides we found moss for the reindeer in the woods," Redmyer recalled. "For miles the forest had recently burned and the trees had fallen in a tangled mass. Through this we had to chop our way. We had to traverse long marshes which were trodden by all the oxen that were sent in to the Klondike."

On September 26, 1898, they arrived at Hoodchee-I, an Indian village. After stocking up on supplies, they took the Selkirk Trail to Ichiaik Lake and followed the mountains toward Circle City.

Snow began in October, and the herders were not prepared for

Woodland Park in Seattle, where the reindeer and herders camped while waiting for transportation to Alaska.

an Alaskan winter. "The Lapps had sent most of their reindeer-skin clothes to St. Michael, and what little outfit I had was almost worn out while being transported on the backs of the reindeer in the heat of the summer, since we had to use the reindeer-skin coat under the pack saddles," Redmyer wrote. "Too, I had to send back the Yukon stove and the best tents for they were too heavy and difficult to pack on the reindeer. I chose the smallest tent to take along. I took this tent and sewed the top in a point, like an Indian teepee. Thus we could have a small fire in the tent and cook our food and at the same time dry our clothes."

They finally reached Dawson City on January 27, 1899. The miners offered to buy the whole herd at $300 apiece for fresh meat, but the herders had to refuse the offer. If they could have sold the animals to a local butcher shop, they would have received approximately $50,000, which would have covered most of the expedition's expenses.

For the next 10 months, the herders moved the reindeer down the Yukon River to Circle City. Stories conflict on what happened after they arrived. One account states that P.C. Richardson, who had a contract for the new mail route from St. Michael to the Dawson goldfields, planned to buy part of the herd. When that did not happen, the deer were driven to the Episcopal mission at St. James and exchanged for does. The mission used the bucks for food and draft purposes, but the account does not mention the does' fates. Another version states that the deer were delivered to several local missions that loaned the animals to rescue whalers stranded in the Arctic Ocean near Point Barrow in the fall of 1897.

Meanwhile, Jackson's Teller Station training program continued. After a slow start, more Eskimos wanted to participate. Within a few years, the program was ruined by its own success. The Eskimos traditionally lived close to the sea, and unlike the Lapps or Siberians, they did not like to follow the herds inland. As the number of reindeer grew, the tundra along the seashore was destroyed.

To alleviate the resulting food shortage, the United States government tried to consolidate the herds into single units for each village. Instead of private, family ownerships with special markings for each owner, each native received a stock certificate. In 1928, a fire destroyed some of the records in the Reindeer Service's office, which caused disputes over ownership. Many Eskimos lost interest, killed the deer for meat, or neglected the herds entirely. Finally, by the 1960s, the herds shrunk almost entirely, and Jackson's training program became only a memory.

References

"A Broadside?" (editorial). *Oregon Journal*, January 19, 1914, p. 5.

Andrews, Clarence L. "Driving Reindeer in Alaska." *Washington Historical Quarterly*, April 1935, pp. 90–93.

Andrews, Clarence L. "Reindeer in Alaska." *Washington Historical Quarterly*, July 1919, pp. 171–186.

Arnst, Albert. "Barn Unique Historical Marker." *Oregon Journal*, June 14, 1962, p. 27.

"Asa Shinn Mercer dies in Nebraska." *Seattle Post-Intelligencer*, August 22, 1917, p. 14.

"Asa Shinn Mercer, Pioneer in Western Publicity." *Pacific Northwest Quarterly*, October 1936, pp. 348–366.

Basic History of Eastern Oregon Counties, 1897. Souvenir edition reprinted in the *Morning Democrat*, Baker City, OR, Christmas 1977.

Bave, Emelia L. *San Juan Saga*. Friday Harbor, WA, 1976.

Bean, Margaret. "Pioneer Doings Relived." *The Spokesman-Review*, September 18, 1945, pp. 1, 4.

Brainard, Wendell. *Golden History Tales from Idaho's Coeur d'Alene Mining District*. Wallace, ID: Crow's Press, 1990.

Blakely, James M. (as told to Herbert Lundy). "Finale...When the Juniper Trees Bore Fruit." *The Oregonian* magazine section, March 26, 1939, p. 8.

Blakely, James M. (as told to Herbert Lundy). "When the Juniper Trees Bore Fruit." *The Oregonian* magazine section, March 12, 1939, pp. 1–2.

Blakely, James M. (as told to Herbert Lundy). "When the Prineville Juniper Trees Bore Fruit." *The Oregonian* magazine section, March 19, 1939, p. 6.

Boone, Lalia. *Idaho Place Names: A Geographical Dictionary*. Moscow, ID:

University of Idaho Press, 1988.
Bragman, Pauline. "Centennial honors Harney Valley rancher." *The Oregonian*, June 25, 1972, p. 26.
Brimlow, George Francis. *Harney County Oregon and its Range Land.* Portland, OR: Binfords and Mort, Publishers, 1951.
Brogan, Phil F. *East of the Cascades.* Portland, OR: Binfords & Mort, Publishers, 1964, pp. 154–161.
Brooke, Leonie N. "Taming the Vagabond Island of the Columbia." *Travel,* July 1942, pp. 9–11, 28.
Brosnan, C.J. *History of the State of Idaho.* New York: Charles Scribner's Sons, 1948.
Bruce, Herbert L. "Republic, the greatest gold camp in Washington." *Seattle Post-Intelligencer,* February 21, 1899, p. 8.
Carlson, L.H. "The First Mining Season at Nome, Alaska—1899." *Pacific Historical Review,* September 1946, pp. 259–278.
Cameron, David. "History: The Greatest Gold Rush of the Cascades." Monte Cristo Preservation Association, http://mcpa.us.
"Carry Nation: American temperance leader." *Encyclopedia Britannica,* n.d., https://www.britannica.com/biography/Carry-Nation.
Coeur d'Alene Mines Corporation website, https://www.coeur.com/overview/default.aspx.
"Columbia island ruling reversed." *The Seattle Times,* April 21, 1896, p. 2.
"Community names: Early-day pioneers/founders left behind a living legacy." *Yodel,* Kellogg, Idaho newspaper, summer 1991, p. 5.
Conover, C.T. "Just Cogitating: Seattle, Victoria short of women in 1860's." *The Seattle Times,* May 2, 1954, magazine section, p. 6.
"Cooperation asked, military law if it is not forthcoming." *Oregon Journal,* January 2, 1914, pp. 1, 9.
"Copperfield" (editorial). *Oregon Journal,* January 9, 1914, p. 8.
"Copperfield in Ruin." *The Oregonian,* August 14, 1915, p. 7.
"Copperfield may be but memory of 'golden days.'" *Oregon Journal,* January 25, 1914, p. 1.
"Copperfield mayor says personal spite is cause of trouble." *Oregon Journal,* January 1, 1914, p. 2.
"Copperfield saloons have got to close." *Oregon Journal,* December 29, 1913, p. 1.
"Crisis near in camp of Copperfield." *Oregon Journal,* January 4, 1914, p. 1.
Courtright, Larry. A *History of Hot Lake Sanatorium.* Typewritten manuscript published June 4, 1965, and housed at Eastern Oregon University Library.
Crystal Gold Mine tour, http://www.goldmine-idaho.com.
Danley, David. Interview, June 1990.

Dodge, Orvil. *The Heroes of Battle Rock.* Typeset booklet, January 1904, housed at the Oregon State Library, Salem, OR.

"Doughface." Wikipedia, September 15, 2024, https://en.wikipedia.org/wiki/Doughface.

Douglas County Museum of History and Natural History, Roseburg, OR.

Douthit, Nathan. *A Guide to Oregon South Coast History.* Coos Bay, OR: River West Books, 1986.

"Drunken boys in saloon of city's chief." *Oregon Journal,* January 8, 1914, pp. 1, 5.

Duff, Marion. "There's New Life in Old Monte Cristo." *The Seattle Times,* August 16, 1964, Charmed Land section, pp. 4–5.

Duncan, Don. "Gold in them thar hills." *Seattle Post-Intelligencer,* April 29, 1969, pp.L1–L2.

Easterling, Jerry. "Former cattle hand rustles up 'interior' memories." *Statesman Journal,* September 12, 1982, p. 3G.

"Edict of martial law is not subject to a review by the court." *Oregon Journal,* January 10, 1914, p. 12.

Engeman, Richard H. *The Jacksonville Story.* Jacksonville, OR: Southern Oregon Historical Society, 1980.

Evans, Gail E.H. *A Walk through Time.* Self-published, date unknown.

Evans, Walter. "The Mercer Girls." *Seattle Post-Intelligencer,* September 7, 1975, "Northwest" section, pp. 6–8.

"Ex-officials arrested at Copperfield." *Oregon Journal,* January 5, 1914, pp. 1–2.

Fleetwood, Leona. Interview, April 1982.

French, Giles. *Cattle Country of Peter French.* Portland, OR: Binfords & Mort, Publishers, 1964.

Friedman, Ralph. "Pete French Left Indelible Mark." *Oregon Journal,* June 7, 1967, p. 12.

Fries, U.E. *From Copenhagen to Okanogan.* Caldwell, ID: Caxton Printers, 1949.

Gibbs, Jim. *Oregon's Salty Coast.* Seattle: Superior Publishing Company, 1978.

Gibson, Wynne. "Ghost Towns of Oregon." *Frontier Times,* April–May 1979, pp. 36–37.

"Governor directs that all Copperfield saloons be closed." *Oregon Journal,* December 22, 1913, p. 3.

"Governor promises 'clean sweep' if the law is not obeyed." *Oregon Journal,* December 23, 1913, p. 4.

"Governor West did right, says Copperfield man." *Oregon Journal,* January 21, 1914, p. 1.

Gray, Edward. *Life and Death of Oregon "Cattle King" Peter French 1849 -*

1897. Salem, OR: Your Town Press, Inc., 1995

Greenhorn City. Typewritten manuscript, date unknown, housed in the Baker County Public Library, Baker City, OR.

Grover, Jack. "Great Oregon Ranch to be Game Refuge." *Oregon Journal*, February 21, 1935, pp. 1, 6.

"Guardsman to enforce law if necessary." *Oregon Journal*, January 2, 1914, pp. 1, 17.

Hardt, Ulrich H. "Shaniko." Oregon Historical Society: Oregon Encyclopedia, n.d., https://www.oregonencyclopedia.org/articles/shaniko.

Historic Jacksonville, Inc. website, https://www.historicjacksonville.org.

History of Baker, Grant, Malheur and Harney Counties. Western Historical Publishing Company, 1902.

Holbrook, Stewart H. *Far Corner: A Personal View of the Pacific Northwest*. New York: The MacMillan Company, 1952, pp. 176–185.

Holman, Alfred. "Monte Cristo Mines." *Seattle Post-Intelligencer*, August 19, 1891, p. 1.

Hug, Bernal D., ed. *History of Union County, Oregon*. La Grande, OR: *Eastern Oregon Review*, 1961, pp. 183–185.

Hull, Lindley. *The History of North Central Washington*. Shaw & Borden, 1929.

Hunt, John Clark. "Story of a Mountain." *American Forests*, September 1960, pp. 34–36, 38–39.

"Idaho Mining Towns." Western Mining History website, https://westernmininghistory.com/state/idaho.

Idaho Power website, https://www.idahopower.com.

Jackman, E.R. and Ray Novotny. "Harney County...Where the 'Wild West' Was Really Wild." *Oregon Farmer*, July 20, 1961, pp. 5, 7–9.

Jackson, Kristin. "An Oregon ghost town evokes Wild West past." *The Seattle Times/Post-Intelligencer*, January 21, 1990, p. J4.

Jacksonville Chamber of Commerce. Jacksonville, Oregon website, http://www.jacksonvilleoregon.org.

"John Randolph and Henry Clay Fight a Duel." EBSCO Knowledge Advantage™, 2022, https://www.ebsco.com/research-starters/history/john-randolph-and-henry-clay-fight-duel.

Johnson, David. "John Randolph of Roanoke" (video lecture). Virginia Museum of History and Culture, 2012, https://virginiahistory.org/learn/john-randolph-roanoke.

Johnson, Jalmar. *Builders of the Northwest*. New York: Dodd, Mead & Company, 1963.

Karolevitz, Bob. "Asa Mercer After Seattle." *The Seattle Times*, March 27, 1966, "Charmed Land" section, page 2.

Kingsnorth, Carolyn. "Mary Ann Harris Chambers – Survivor." *Jacksonville*

Review, March 1, 2018, https://jacksonvillereview.com/mary-ann-harris-chambers-survivor-carolyn-kingsnorth.

Kirkpatrick, Terry. "Greed, fear put the luster on gold." *The Spokesman Review*, December 9, 1979, pp. 13–14.

Kittredge, William. "Natural Causes." *American West*, September/October 1983, pp. 48–54.

Klondike Silver Corporation website, https://klondikesilver.com.

KSPS PBS Public TV. "Silver Linings: The Early History of Idaho's Silver Valley," https://www.youtube.com/watch?v=UOaC3OzpkT0&t=2s

Landes, Henry. *Preliminary report on the underground waters of Washington*. University of Washington, n.d., pp. 17–20.

"Lawyer represents state in injunction hearing at Baker." *Oregon Journal*, January 10, 1914, p. 1.

"Lee Sutton Recalls the 1903 Sheep Massacre." *Okanogan County Heritage*, March 1967, pp. 31–32.

Lewis, Loretta. "History of Ruby City: The Life and Death of a Mining Town." *Pacific Northwest Quarterly*, January 1941, pp. 61–78.

Lippman, Wendy. "The hours pass peacefully at Monte Cristo." *Seattle Post-Intelligencer*, December 20, 1981, "Northwest People" section, pp. 14–15.

"Living Ghosts." *Argus*, August 31, 1973, p. 4.

"Local Intelligence" (message from Mercer). *Puget Sound Weekly*, May 14, 1866, p. 4.

Lockley, Fred. "Men and Institutions of Oregon Country." *Oregon Journal*, March 27- 31, 1919.

Luke, Stella. *100 Years of Mining*. Publisher unknown, ca. 1990.

Magnuson, Richard G. *Coeur d'Alene Diary*. Portland, OR: Binford and Mort Publishing, 1968.

Markle, Richard. "Shaniko." *Frontier Times*, Winter 1961, pp. 56–57.

McDonald, Lucile. "Okanogan County had its own Christmas 'Baby.'" *The Seattle Times*, December 20, 1964, p. 7.

McDonald. Lucile. "Old Mining Center Hopes to Build Future on Uranium." *The Seattle Times*, September 8, 1957, p. 2.

McDonald, Lucile. "Ruins of Old Vault at Conconully Recall Era When Town Was Okanogan County Seat." *The Seattle Times*, March 2, 1958, p. 2.

McNamer, Deirdre. "Shaniko Hotel: A Place and People Out of Time." *Oregon Times Magazine*, March 1977, pp. 41–47.

Menefee, Leah Collins, and Tiller, Lowell. "Cutoff Fever" (series of articles on Elliott wagon train published in the *Oregon Historical Quarterly*) December 1976, pp. 309–349; March 1977, pp. 41–72; June 1977, pp. 121–157; September 1977, pp. 207–250; December 1977, pp.

293–331; Spring 1978, pp. 5–50.
"Mercer's Speech." *Puget Sound Weekly*, May 28, 1866, p. 6.
"Merchant gets 'black hand' card." *Oregon Journal*, December 27, 1913, p. 1.
"Militia and Citizens Rule Copperfield." *Oregon Journal*, January 3, 1914, p. 1.
"Miss Fern Hobbs not frightened but real 'mad.'" *Oregon Journal*, January 3, 1914, pp. 1–2.
"Miss Hobbs anxious to get to work and out of limelight." *Oregon Journal*, January 5, 1914, pp. 1–2.
"Miss Hobbs' new job is to 'clean up' Copperfield." *Oregon Journal*, December 30, 1913, pp. 1, 4.
"Mine to Market Road Expected to Help Monte Cristo to Come Back." *Everett Daily Herald*, January 26, 1950, p. 25.
"Monte Cristo: Ghost town with a future." *Seattle Post-Intelligencer*, December 16, 1988, p. C2.
"Monte Cristo Mines. Story of Their Discovery by Joe Pearsall." *Seattle Post-Intelligencer*, September 26, 1892, p. 8.
Montgomery, Jerry. "Vandals, heavy snows again damage Monte Cristo site." *The Seattle Times*, August 6, 1972, p. E9.
Montgomery, Maurice. "The Murder of Missionary Thornton." *Pacific Northwest Quarterly*, October 1963, pp. 167–174.
Moore, Anne Shannon. "Pete French: Oregon's Cattle King Who 'Had to Be Killed.'" *The Oregonian*, April 14, 1935, magazine section, pp. 1, 5.
Moore, Anne Shannon. "The Strange Fate..." *The Oregonian*, April 21, 1935, magazine section, p.4.
Morrison, Eula Atwood. "Old Mining Center is in Spotlight Again." *The Seattle Times*, December 5, 1954, p. 2.
"Mrs. Harris." Southern Oregon History, *Revised*, June 7, 2025, https://truwe.sohs.org/files/mrs.harris.html.
Mt. Baker-Snoqualmie National Forest. *Monte Cristo Historical Tour*. U.S. Department of Agriculture, Pacific Northwest Region, n.d., https://npshistory.com/publications/usfs/region/6/mount-baker-snoqualmie/monte-cristo-historical-tour.pdf.
Murray, Keith. *The Pig War*. Tacoma, WA: Washington State Historical Society, April 1968.
Murray, Keith A. *Reindeer and Gold*. Bellingham, WA: Center for Pacific Northwest Studies, Western Washington University, August 1988.
Needham, Gordon. *Official Map and Handbook of the Coeur d'Alene Mines*. Fairfield, WA: Ye Galleon Press, 1884, reprinted 1988.
Nogaki, Sylvia Wieland. "U.S., Canada in second Pig War." *The Seattle Times*, September 26, 1989, pp. F1, F6.

"Not a drop of hard liquor in Copperfield." *Oregon Journal,* January 6, 1914, pp. 1–2.

Okanogan County, Washington Genealogy and History. *Genealogy Trails,* March 1, 2006, https://genealogytrails.com/wash/okanogan/bios.html.

Oregon Parks and Recreation Division, State Historic Preservation Office. Statements of historical significance for Hot Lake property.

Pellowski, Veronika. *Silver, Lead, and Hell: The Story of Sandon.* Sandon, BC: Prospectors' Pick Publishing, 1992.

Peterson, Emil R. and Alfred Powers. *A Century of Coos and Curry.* Portland, OR: Binfords & Mort, Publishers, 1952.

Peterson, F. Ross. Idaho: *A Bicentennial History.* New York: W.W. Norton and Company, Inc., 1976.

Picken, Nellie B. "Cowboy tales from the Okanogan." *The Spokesman-Review,* February 3, 1952, magazine section, p. 8.

Port Orford Chamber of Commerce. Battle of Battle Rock brochure. Port Orford, OR, n.d.

Potter, Miles, *Oregon's Golden Years.* Caldwell, ID: Caxton Press, 1975.

Propster, Lt. Col. Howard A. "The Story of Soap Lake, Washington." *Washington Wonderland,* March 1962, pp. 7–10.

Pryne, Eric. "Counting on Monte Cristo." *The Seattle Times,* February 7, 1993, pp. A1, A14–15.

Quesnell, Bart. "Mystique of a mining town." *The Spokesman-Review Progress Issue,* Spokane, Washington newspaper, December 10, 1979, pp. 89–90.

Rascoe, Burton. *The Great Trek,* 1935.

Ray, Dorothy Jean. "Sheldon Jackson and the Reindeer Industry of Alaska." *Journal of Presbyterian History,* June 1965, pp. 71–99.

Redmyer, Hedley E. "Reindeer in Alaska (reprint of letter to editor of *Skandinaven,* dated June 5, 1899)." *Pacific Northwest Quarterly,* July 1951, pp. 215–223.

Rees, Helen Guyton. *Shaniko: From Wool Capital to Ghost Town.* Portland, OR: Binford and Mort Publishing, 1982.

Rees, Helen Guyton. *Shaniko People.* Portland, OR: Binford and Mort Publishing, 1983.

"Republic, a camp that came back." *Seattle Post-Intelligencer,* June 30, 1912, p. 1.

"Republic suffers a disastrous fire." *Seattle Post-Intelligencer,* June 4, 1899, p. 1.

Richard, Terry. "Hot Lake Springs about to be reborn." *The Oregonian,* July 13, 2008, https://www.oregonlive.com/terryrichard/2008/07/hot_lake_springs_about_to_be_r.html.

Richardson, David. *Pig War Islands*. Eastsound, WA: Orcas Publishing Co., 1971.

Roth, Richard R. *Hot Lake: A Short Story, 2nd Edition*. Orting, WA: Heritage Quest Press, n.d.

Roth, Richard R. *The Hot Lake Story*. Orting, WA: Heritage Quest Press, 2008.

Roth, Richard R. *The Hot Lake Story: Heritage Supplement*. Orting, WA: Heritage Quest Press, 2012.

Schwartz, E.A. "Rogue River War of 1855-1856." Oregon Historical Society: Oregon Encyclopedia, n.d., https://www.oregonencyclopedia.org/articles/rogue_river_war_of_1855-1856.

"Seattle has awakened to the riches of Republic." *Seattle Post-Intelligencer*, February 14, 1899, p. 11.

"Sheriff Rand asks criticism withheld." *Oregon Journal*, December 24, 1913, p. 3.

"Sheriff Rand on his way to Copperfield." *Oregon Journal*, January 7, 1914, p. 1.

Shimanek, Jo. "The Hot Lake..." *Observer Progress Report*, 1969, Section A, p. 4.

Silversmith Power & Light Corporation. *Interpretive Guide*. Sandon, BC, 2017.

Simons, Audrey. "Oregon's Former 'Wool Capital Of The World' Is A Once-Abandoned Ghost Town Reborn With Shops And A Hotel." *Islands*, August 1, 2025, https://www.islands.com/1922510/shaniko-oregon-former-wool-capital-once-abandoned-ghost-town-reborn-shops-hotel.

Simpson, Peter K. *The Community of Cattlemen*. Moscow: ID: University of Idaho Press, 1987.

Soap Lake Chamber of Commerce. *The Story of Soap Lake*. Typewritten manuscript published in 1976 with support from the Washington State American Revolution Bicentennial Commission and the Soap Lake Bicentennial Committee.

Statue of Liberty-Ellis Island Foundation, Inc. website, https://www.statueofliberty.org.

Stevens, Harriet F. "Communicated" (letter). *Puget Sound Weekly*, June 4, 1866, p. 3.

Stewart, Bill. "Small gold mine enjoys a rebirth." *The Spokesman Review*, December 9, 1979, p. 13.

Stewart, George. "Tragedies of a mining town." *B.C. Outdoors*, November–December 1969, pp. 22–27.

Stewart, Gordon and Patricia. *Baker County Sketchbook*. Baker City, OR: Baker County Chamber of Commerce, 1956.

"Stockmen of Early Days in Harney." *Oregon Journal*, June 13, 1932, p. 6.

Stokes, Ted. "Sand Island: The Second War Between the States." *Oregon Coast*, March/April 1990, pp. 15–16.

Strathorn, Robert E. *The Resources and Attractions of Idaho Territory.* Moscow, ID: University of Idaho Press, 1881, reprinted 1990.

Stripling, Sherry. "Mercer the Matchmaker." *Seattle Post-Intelligencer*, February 12, 1984, pp. 17–19.

Sunriver Nature Center, Sunriver, OR.

"The Breakout of '55." Southern Oregon History, *Revised*, October 25, 2024, https://truwe.sohs.org/files/breakout.html.

"The Copperfield Affair." *The Sunday Oregonian Magazine*, April 20, 1952, pp. 8–9.

Thompson, Sabrina. "A new chapter for Hot Lake Springs." *The Observer*, November 3, 2020, https://lagrandeobserver.com/2020/11/03/a-new-chapter-for-hot-lake-springs.

Thompson, William. *Reminiscences of a Pioneer.* San Francisco, 1912, pp. 167–174.

Todd, Ronald. "The Steamer 'Beaver.'" *Pacific Northwest Quarterly*, October 1936, pp. 367–368.

Town and Country Forum. *History Report.* Typewritten history of Soap Lake published in April 1958 and housed at the Grant County Historical Society, Ephrata, Washington.

"Town of Republic Grows." *Seattle Post-Intelligencer*, May 10, 1898, p. 11.

Turnbull, Elsie G. "Frontier hotels in Kootenay country." *B.C. Outdoors*, September–October 1976, pp. 14–21.

Turnbull, Elsie G. "Poplar Creek and the Colonel of the Kootenays." *B.C. Outdoors*, September-October 1974, pp. 18–23.

U.S. Bank of Oregon. "Historic Jacksonville." Brochure describing historic sites in Jacksonville, date unknown.

U.S. Department of Transportation, Federal Highway Administration. "A Look at the History of the Federal Highway Administration. FHWA By Day - September 12," http://www.fhwa.dot.gov/byday/fhbd0912.htm.

Varriano, Jackie. "Why you should visit Oregon's oldest resort." *The Seattle Times*, July 4, 2025, https://www.seattletimes.com/life/travel/why-you-should-visit-oregons-oldest-resort.

Ward, Beverly. *White Moccasins.* Myrtle Point, OR: Myrtle Point Printing, 1986.

Warren, James. "Mercer imported wives for Seattle pioneer men." *Seattle Post-Intelligencer*, May 13, 1987, pp. C2, C7.

"Washington man was 19th-century adventurer and traveler." *Seattle Post-Intelligencer*, April 29, 1969, pp. L1–L2.

Weather and terrain descriptions in Eastern Oregon are from my personal experiences. I lived in Eastern Oregon for four years.

Webb, Novus. *Backyard Mining in Jacksonville.* Jacksonville, OR: Southern Oregon Historical Society, 1979.

Webber, Bert (ed.). *The Hero of Battle Rock.* Fairfield, WA: Ye Galleon Press, 1973.

Webber, Bert and Margie. *Jacksonville: The Making of a National Historic Landmark.* Fairfield, WA: Ye Galleon Press, 1983.

Wells, Gail. "The Oregon Coast—'Forists and Green Verdent Launs': Mining, Lumbering, and Shipbuilding." Oregon Historical Society, Oregon History Project, n.d., https://www.oregonhistoryproject.org/narratives/the-oregon-coastforists-and-green-verdent-launs/development-of-the-coastal-economy/mining-lumbering-and-shipbuilding.

West, Oswald. "French-Glenn Lands Purchased By Federal Government for Game Refuge." *The Oregon Democrat,* June 21, 1935, pp. 4, 14.

"West upheld in action at Copperfield." *Oregon Journal,* January 15, 1914, p. 1.

Whitfield, William. *History of Snohomish County, Washington.* Chicago: Pioneer Historical Publishing Company, 1926.

Wilkie, Rosemary. *A Broad Bold Ledge of Gold.* Seattle: Shorey Book Store, 1973.

Winters, Matt. "Sand Islands: A mystery in plain sight." *The Astorian,* March 25, 2014, https://dailyastorian.com/2014/03/25/sand-islands-a-mystery-in-plain-sight.

Wiseman, Joe. "Crossed Sherman Pass in 1896; Saw Republic Grow." *Republic (Wn) News-Miner,* August 28, 1953, p. 12.

"Within the law" (editorial). *Oregon Journal,* January 20, 1914, p. 6.

Woodbury, Chuck. "'Ghost' hotel returns to life." *Out West,* Fall 1988, p. 12.

Index

D

E

F

G

H

N

O

P

R

S

X

Y

Acknowledgments

Special thanks go to Annette Hall, whose eagle eyes picked up many things in this manuscript that I missed because I was too close to it; and to Laura Stone, whose artistic talents helped me get out of design trouble on the book cover. Also, special thanks go to Leona Fleetwood, the niece of former Greenhorn mayor Simeon C. Richardson, who welcomed a 22-year-old college student into her home in Baker City and spent the entire day reminiscing about life in Greenhorn when it was a booming mining town. Not only did she vividly describe her experiences there, but she also told some interesting stories about Baker City and the entire county. Her stories became ideas for chapters in this book and magazine articles.

Thank you to Al Smith, a photographer who reprinted historical pictures I ordered through the Oregon State Library. An amateur historian and long-time resident of Salem, he voluntarily enclosed additional reference materials in the packages of photos he mailed to me. I learned a lot about Northwest history from our correspondence.

For all the librarians and staff at these historical societies, libraries, and museums throughout the Northwest, thank you for your assistance in pulling items from the archives and directing me to information I hadn't considered in my research:

- Baker County Public Library
- British Columbia Archives and Records Service
- Coos Bay Public Library
- Deschutes County Historical Society
- Douglas County Historical Society
- Eastern Oregon University Library

- Oregon Historical Society
- Lane County Historical Museum
- Marion County Historical Society
- Okanogan County Historical Society
- Oregon State Library
- Salem Public Library
- Sandon Historical Museum
- Seattle Public Library
- Southern Oregon Historical Society
- Sumpter Valley Museum
- Union County Museum
- University of Idaho Library
- University of Oregon Libraries
- University of Washington Libraries
- Washington State Historical Society

And thank you to Nancy Stohlman and everyone in The Flash Fiction Mastermind Community for encouraging me to finish the second edition of this book. Although these stories are non-fiction, you all helped me keep going. I'm grateful for your cheerleading and friendship.

The Power of the Pen online meetup, hosted by Andrew Zimmerman, has also been a vital source of encouragement and support. Thank you, Andrew, for hosting these weekly events.

Another thank-you goes to HR Hegnauer, who set up the eBook version of this second edition. I'm grateful for your help and support.

Last but not least, I want to thank my family and friends not listed here for your encouragement and support. I love you all.

About the Author

Cheryl Landes is a communications consultant, freelance travel writer, and the author of *The Best I Can Do*, *Rainbows in the Snow*, *Beautiful America's Seattle* (two editions), *Beautiful America's Idaho*, and *Those Wild Northwest Days*. Her articles and essays have appeared in national and regional publications, from *HuffPost* to *Sunset*, and on her Tabby Cat's Pawprints blog. She has also contributed chapters about findability to *The Language of Content Strategy* and *The Language of Technical Communication*.

She volunteers on the marketing and events committees at Animal Aid, a no-kill shelter founded in 1969 in Portland, Oregon; and teaches Family to Family classes for the Southwest Washington affiliate of the National Alliance on Mental Illness (NAMI).

Cheryl lives in Vancouver, Washington, where she enjoys photography, hiking, listening to music, reading, and hanging out with cats (with their permission, of course).

Visit Cheryl's website at tabbycatco.com and her travel blog at tabbycatspawprints.com.

www.ingramcontent.com/pod-product-compliance
Lightning Source LLC
LaVergne TN
LVHW090514110826
845146LV00003B/855

* 9 7 9 8 9 8 9 5 4 5 0 4 9 *